FIND YOUR INNER
SUPER G

GINA M. MULLIS

authorHOUSE®

AuthorHouse™
1663 Liberty Drive
Bloomington, IN 47403
www.authorhouse.com
Phone: 1 (800) 839-8640

Published by AuthorHouse 01/17/2018

ISBN: 978-1-5462-2383-2 (sc)
ISBN: 978-1-5462-2382-5 (e)

Library of Congress Control Number: 2018900183

Print information available on the last page.

Contents

Thank you to my friends and family, to my support team. You strengthened me. You empowered me. I am forever grateful! To you, the reader, I truly believe you can achieve whatever it is you seek. Hard times, your past, naysayers, nothing at all can hold you back. Don't ever give up.

This book is dedicated to the best companion and "little brother" anyone could ask for, Major Abraham Lincoln Lee. RIP, Lincoln, Sissy loves you always.

Cover Photo courtesy of Michael Gray Photography: www.michaelgrayphotography.com

Visit www.ginamullis.com for exclusive Empowerment Program extras! Visit www.amerie.org to #ShopWithPurpose

Foreword

It may sound crazy, but I am beyond grateful for the series of unfortunate events that have fallen upon me in life. My newfound skill of finding appreciation, knowledge, and wisdom from both positive and challenging experiences is one I cherish. I want nothing more than to share that invaluable tool with others in hopes that they too can find happiness, joy, and peace in the aftermath of tragedy and remain humble when riding the waves of greatness and success. I have always believed that every person possesses good but must cultivate and nurture it in order for it to radiate. Some choose to snuff out the goodness within them completely, some allow defeat to snuff it out, and others choose to let it shine for the world to see. It can feel impossible at times to remain positive and radiate light and positive energy when nothing is going your way. Life has its way of weighing us down sometimes, but I believe you can feel joy. You can accomplish your goals and reach your dreams, even those that seem out of reach. You can become that person you wish you were. You can live with true happiness in your heart. You can find success.

You already know life is short, and you know that tomorrow is never guaranteed. Sometimes it takes eye opening moments, usually tragic or challenging ones, for us to truly understand. I was lucky enough to have that moment (more than one, actually). Yes, I said I was lucky to have a tragedy. I am stronger. I am wiser. I am more selfless, more self-aware, and living life with more intention than ever before because of those life-changing moments. You too can gain wisdom and knowledge, find true happiness, and become the person you are meant to be, and I want to help you on your journey. I want to empower you, inspire you, and motivate you. Parts of this empowerment program may not apply to you and some you may need to revisit often. Either way, I believe you can and will reach your potential and live a happy and successful life, and I will do what I can to help you!

Step One

Understanding yourself, your goals, and beginning to grow in the right direction.

Part 1

The Reason Why

Here's Why. Are you living in slow motion, have experienced some life-changing event, are in a slump of some sort, or are just ready to take your life to the next level? I think the majority of people, at some point in life, have a moment where they wonder "what if?" They wonder how life would be different if they had gone to college, or waited to have kids, or if they would have studied abroad for a year. Some may consider this notion a mid-life crisis of sorts, but I don't like calling it a crisis for the mere fact that I truly believe every single person has that thought, "what if?" therefore, it isn't truly a crisis but more a commonality, a shared life check-point even. Heck, if you're like me you may even sometimes contemplate how today would be different if you would have eaten healthier yesterday or washed your hair earlier so you could have more time to relax later. Little 'what ifs' are normal, and so are big ones. Some may disagree, but I am here to assure you that it is okay, acceptable, expected, and normal to have a "what if" moment in your life, many of them, in fact. Knowing how to handle those moments and turn them into something great is the true challenge and meaning of life.

Before we move on, it's perfectly fine if you have no idea exactly what you want to do in life, but it never hurts to continuously consider possibilities (which is one thing you will do throughout this book!). In this Part, you will glimpse several aspects necessary in your life journey before moving on to Parts that dig deeper into each concept. Some principals overlap at times because they are important and usable in varying ways. Each person possesses individualized life goals, ideas, and experiences, so it is perfectly acceptable if you don't relate to every single aspect of this program. Use what you need. Use what helps you grow and adds value to your journey.

Now, try jotting down some thoughts. Write some things you hope to accomplish in life. Maybe you hope to get married or become a parent. Maybe you hope to become a police officer or business owner. Maybe you want to travel or coach a team. Just because you write it down doesn't mean you can't change your mind later. Also, write for yourself. We aren't focusing on what your parents, your spouse, or anyone else wants for you.

I'd like to one day accomplish the following:

Are you a high school student? In your thirties? Are you a grandmother of four? It doesn't matter your age, nor does it matter where you have been before and what you have done, or haven't done. In fact, those experiences will help you, you'll see. So, the purpose for unlocking your true potential is simple: You get one life, and you want it to be the best one it can possibly be; you want it to be a happy one. Once you unlock that something lurking deep down within you, that passion, that thing that ignites you, your "what ifs" will no longer feel painful or regretful. Instead, they will act as new ideas or projects, new inspiration, and new goals! Our goal (yours and mine) by reading this and working through the empowerment program, is to do just that: empower. Every human is born with qualities necessary to become happy and successful in life, but it's sometimes difficult to find the correct path, make the right choices, or just know how to begin to get where you desire to be. I want you to find the inspiration, feel the empowerment it takes to really start making things happen!

"Every human is born with qualities necessary to become happy and successful in life..."

Think of qualities you possess, not skills you have learned, but personality traits or things about you that make you who you are. *For example: I am creative. I am outgoing. I am goofy and funny.*

<u>**List 3 or more qualities you possess that
others would recognize in you.**</u>

Now, think for a moment of how any one of those qualities would be useful to you in your efforts to reach your goals. Together we can make the necessary connections to create a clear path for you to follow, making your journey to happiness clearer and more travelable.

Create your Road Map. Another reason you are here reading this is so you and I can create a road map to your success. First, and sometimes the most challenging step, you must create a guide and have vision. I have learned through a variety of experiences that it is a fantastic idea to plan things. Plan your vacation, plan what you want to do after graduation, plan your meals for the week. Planning makes things a little easier and less stressful, unless they go completely wrong. A derailed plan can really bring a person down and cause chaos. So, I started creating road maps for various aspects of my life. Like a plan, a road map provides a clear guide for you to follow. Unlike a plan, a road map shows more than one path all leading to the same destination, so I can choose a destination on the map and choose which route I hope to take to reach my destination, but if there is a detour I can easily find an alternate route. Much the same, you can bank on snagging that dream job you applied for, but what happens if you don't get the job? You must have plans, goals, dreams, but you must also possess the flexibility needed when things don't work out as you thought they would. A road map allows you an opportunity to view a let down, such as not getting that job, as an opening to take a different path where you will experience things you otherwise may not have. It's a simple mind trick to think of life's curve balls as positive rather than as a failed plan.

As you progress through this book and work toward drafting a plan to accomplish your aspirations, please remember some dreams are more difficult to reach than others, and some take more time to reach than others. Sometimes accomplishing a task is only somewhat in our own control. Oftentimes, we have to put in the work to get what we want, but others involved also have to cooperate. You may want nothing more than anything to get that job you applied for, but even if you are the perfect candidate for the position it comes down to someone else deciding whether you will reach that goal. A flexible road map would allow you to regroup and figure out your next steps toward reaching that goal, should it not work out exactly as planned the first time. Defeat and setbacks are just a part of what every single person encounters throughout life, but it does not mean a dream is dead and can never be accomplished. You just have to understand how to learn from each moment and grow in order to travel on.

You may also be working with several roadmaps at once. Maybe you are writing a book in hopes of reaching your dream of becoming a published author and meanwhile are working toward getting a promotion at your job. Those are two separate goals with different routes to get to each, and you can travel both paths at once. In fact, I encourage you to reach for any and all ambitions you can conjure if they make you happy, but we will talk more about that later.

Use Your Tools. I want to help you discover value in the tools you already have! Whether you are a high school student, in college, or in your sixties, you already possess important knowledge and skills to get you where you hope to go in life. Important skills can be hidden in the things we do in life that we don't even realize have any connection with what we want to be doing. For example, a person working at a fast food restaurant is gaining important communication skills, teamwork skills, customer service skills, and more. Whether the person enjoys working in the restaurant business or not, he will gain so much necessary knowledge and so many useful tools to help him succeed with future endeavors. Your goal may be to climb a corporate ladder or own and operate your own business someday, but all the experiences you have prior to accomplishing those goals are vital. So, if you remember anything from reading this remember to cherish and gain from every experience because each one is a step closer to your destination.

What are your skills?

Take a moment and think of things you are good at, skills you have. These are things you have learned over time or skills and knowledge you have had to work a little to build, improve, and shape. *For example: I am a skilled basketball coach. I am skilled at keyboarding/typing. I am knowledgeable with accounting and finance.*

What are you good at? Skilled at? Knowledgeable about? Write some thoughts down here:

Don't underestimate the skills you have. You don't have to be a college graduate or even a high school one to be intelligent or talented. Everyone is knowledgeable about things and knows little about other things, and we all have room to continue learning, always. I hope you begin to realize that gaining skills and knowledge is literally all around us all the time. Every experience from the ten minutes you stand in line to get coffee to the four years you spend attending college, all the negative experiences and positive ones, every single thing we do, see, and hear is a useful learning opportunity.

Be a Leader. You were born with qualities that hold the potential to allow you to become an effective leader. Through this program you will learn what specific qualities of highly effective leaders are and how finding the leader within you is so important in reaching the success you seek. No matter what your definition of success is and what your life goals are, you need to become the best leader you possibly can, which requires an understanding of the many types of leadership and which type you are. One of the objectives of this program is to generate contagious empowerment, and part of your success and happiness is finding the leader in you.

Be Fearless. Another purpose of this program is to encourage you to become fearless in order to become the most extraordinary version of yourself. Once you find the freedom and courage to just go for it, you will feel a rush of inspiration and determination, the kind necessary to make things happen!

Who is this program for? To be completely honest, the information in this program has taken me years (32 to be exact) of experiences, observations, trial and error, and life to learn. It is the type of dry-cut guidance I wish I had at my disposal long ago, and it is right for anyone who wants to be the best possible version of themselves. I don't know anyone who doesn't want to feel happiness and passion about life. This program is right for the dreamers just needing a little help grasping that dream. More specifically, the following examples may provide a more concrete answer to who this program is for:

- Anyone seeking more out of life
- Anyone wishing to get promoted in a career
- Anyone desiring respect from others
- Anyone who wants genuine happiness
- Anyone who has had setbacks or fallen upon tough times, and is seeking inspiration to move forward.
- Anyone unsure of what steps to take next
- Anyone searching for focus or guidance to help move them in a direction toward success
- Anyone learning to trust again
- Anyone learning to let go of anger and doubt
- Anyone ready for a change

How can Super G help? A group of former colleagues from a job I started in 2014, a group who I now consider family because of the many life-changing experiences they were by my side through, gave me the nickname *Super G*. One co-worker in particular was known to hand out nicknames, and I earned mine from him during my newfound battle with Multiple Sclerosis. I remain close with these friends. Like I said, they are family, and I have since transformed my nickname into a way of life and a metaphor to help others gain the insight I have since found. Essentially, Super G represents a determination and will to continue pushing forward, helping others, and reaching goals even when the odds seemed to all stack against me. Super heroes possess special powers that allow them to defeat evil, do great things, and be good humans. While

I don't have any supernatural powers, I do have something extra special that has allowed me to understand something some never will: How to be extraordinary. You too have that ability! This program will allow you to realize what your super powers are and guide you to finding the *Super G* in you!

I thank the variety of life experiences, mixed with personal qualities and shaped skills for the empowerment I now hold. I have years of experience in teaching and learning. I taught middle and high school English Language Arts for six and a half years, own a business that works with over fifteen non-profits every single year to give back to the community and has given back over $30,000 in just two years, have coached for over nine years, a marriage and divorce, and have a devastating Multiple Sclerosis diagnosis under my belt. Every single one of us has our own resume full of important life moments, and I hope you will realize how valuable each one of those items is to you. I want every single person to hone the skill of finding wisdom from downfall, happiness from the small things, and the motivation and determination to full-force obtain total happiness and joy.

The first thing I need you to do is identify your current status, what got you to this point, why are you ready for change? Did you lose a job, graduate school, experience a tragedy, why are you ready for more? This isn't necessarily a negative thing, but is just a time for a change, a new chapter.

Write your thoughts here:

You must also identify what it is you are searching for. Maybe you had a dream as a child that you are realizing never left you. Maybe you are unhappy and seeking pure happiness. Perhaps you are tired of struggling or realized recently that our time on Earth is limited and you have goals you still hope to reach. Whatever you are going through, whatever your reason for readiness to grow, it is a valid one that should be embarked upon!

To begin, you must free your mind of clutter and think one task at a time. Don't allow yourself to feel overwhelmed. Now, revisit the basics. Peel away anything you have been through, any negative thoughts you have, and any doubts, and just remember that thing that you are seeking. You have dreams and aspirations that you want so badly, but try and focus on the root to your dreams and that will generate happiness for you. Together we can, step by step, work toward conquering those tasks. I will be your advocate, your cheerleader, because I believe you can achieve anything and reach those dreams.

Are you thinking to yourself that your dreams are impossible? If not, good! They are not impossible. Realistically, some things we want to accomplish so badly at a young age do become impossible. A tone deaf person is, realistically, less likely to become a famous singer, for example. Or maybe you experienced something that changed the path of your dreams. For example, your dream as a youth was to run a race in the Olympic Games, but you were prevented from doing so when you became paralyzed in a horrific accident. No, you will most likely never compete as a runner in the Olympics, but that dream is not dead. Go back to the basics. Your initial spark was to be a runner then later grew into a dream to race in the Olympics. Your passion is for running. All you have to do is revisit that true passion and foundation of the dreams you have. If you are certainly incapable of completing the goal, as in this example, think of new and similar dreams that stem from your same passion. If you are truly passionate about something you will still find joy in them even in a different capacity. In this example, the person who is wheelchair bound may decide to participate in the variety of national and world competitions specifically for those in wheelchairs. Those competitions are equally as challenging, if not more, and as respected and honored. This same person with a passion for running may choose to train individuals who have potential to themselves become Olympic runners, or even become a coach, trainer, or involved in some capacity in coaching an Olympic running team.

The possibilities are endless if you just get back to the root, the basic flame that is the true passion within you. So, regardless of your confidence in your ability to reach your goals and live your dreams, believe me when I say you can and will achieve them and find happiness.

Part 2

Unlocking your Potential

What is Potential? When we are young (and you may still be) we hear people tell us (or wish they would) what great potential we have. I remember someone telling me a million years ago when I was around eight years old that I had musical potential. I don't even remember who it was, but I think it was someone from the church band or choir. Those simple words inspired me to sing in the church choir and join the school band, and I am thankful for those experiences. Am I a famous singer or musician? No. Do I want to be? No, but I learned so much from those involvements. Potential is the natural mixture of qualities, traits, and skills each of us possess that, if acted upon, can create greatness in a particular skill or expertise. You may have the potential to break defensive line records on your school's football team. If that is the case, you could later go on to show potential to break state records or college or NFL records. Potential is limitless because it all depends how much we nurture and build upon it. If your potential is something you are passionate about and care about the possibilities are endless, and it is up to you how far you want to go with it!

Potential is a combination of personality traits, skills, passion or interest, and hard work. I may have the potential to be the best card house builder in the world, but if I have zero desire to try or build upon that potential, it will never grow into an accomplishment, and that is fine. You get to choose what your hard work and focus will be awarded to. Whatever your passion is, that fire that gets you excited about life, you can make a successful life out of it in some capacity. All you have to do is unlock what that passion is and explore what potential you have that feeds that passion, as well as ways to turn it into greatness you can make a life out of.

You have a choice. It is a choice to either use every experience as a tool to better yourself and move you toward happiness or to give in to hardships, give up, and settle on something less than your dream. I, personally, choose to live, to be a good person, to do good things, and to be strong. You are manager of how you choose to spend your days on earth, whether it's by providing a useful service, creating things, providing entertainment, sharing or teaching skills or knowledge, or anything else you yearn to do. All you have to do is take the necessary steps to discover every inch of your greatness and how to shape and use it to your benefit.

The Potential is there…How do I Unlock it? Before you can truly unlock your potential to be successful, you have to define what that means. To be clear, success looks different to each person, so you cannot check the dictionary to learn what success is. Instead, you will need to assess your life, your goals and dreams, and determine what would make you happiest above all else. Success is once you have reached a goal and are living a life you truly love. There are different types of success that you may experience throughout life, smaller accomplishments and larger ones, but let's talk overall life happiness success. So, you have to figure out what would make you truly happy. Some people desire only money, and for them success may be making billions of dollars each year, though you may find even with endless funds you long for something else in addition. Others view success as having a happy and healthy family or living a life of servitude driven by helping others. You may even combine more than one idea of success to determine what your definition is. Once you figure out what your gauge of personal success will be, you can start figuring out how to reach it.

Let's interact: *For me, at this moment in my life, success is owning and growing my own business with a focus and mission on: helping others; educating others; making a positive impact in my community; bringing awareness to vital causes and organizations; remaining healthy; and inspiring others.*

Take a moment to consider what some concepts of success are for you. What are things you haven't yet accomplished but are working toward or would like to work toward that you would consider great success that bring happiness to you? Write some thoughts below:

Personal Growth. Unlocking your potential requires continuous personal growth. Transform yourself into the kind of person you admire and respect, a human who feels good and makes others feel the same. Growing isn't strictly a physical thing, it means renovating your inner self by learning and experiencing. Like an architectural beauty, you too should always be changing, holding memories and experiences, updating, and renovating; the original frame and best qualities are still there but with improvements.

When humans go through significant experiences they tend to, in ways, change within. Someone who goes through a battle with cancer may experience newfound feelings of strength, hope, or even sadness or defeat, and during and after that experience that person will always have that memory, for example. Those are called life-changing events for a reason: they change the people affected. While some situations are beyond our control, we still often have a choice of what to take away from the event, what to learn from it, or how it will affect us. That small amount of control provides us with a priceless opportunity to learn and grow in ways that will help shape us into better, stronger, wiser, more resourceful, and even happier people.

There are also voluntary growth moments available to you every single day. Think of something you did today, whether it was wait in a drive-thru for breakfast, go to the gym, or see co-workers or classmates in the lounge. Now think about any interaction required during those instances and how you acted or reacted, how others involved acted or reacted, what was said and done. Now consider the following:

Could you have said or done something differently to improve the situation?

Could others involved have said or done something different to better the situation?

Was there anything about the other people involved that you noticed or admired?

Is there anything at all you can take away from that moment to add more value to your bank of skills or experiences?

For example, this morning while getting coffee at a local coffee shop a woman standing in line complimented my old, worn-looking boots. I did not know the woman, and my boots, though stylish, are visibly old and worn. I looked at the woman carefully as I thanked her for the compliment and noticed many things I could compliment her on. Not wanting her to think I was only complimenting her on something because she had done it first, I simply nodded with a smile and look of approval at her much cuter-than-mine shoes and said, "Trade ya!" We both chuckled and smiled, and I left the shop. What I took from that situation is the slightly happier mood I felt when she complimented me and a hunger to cause someone else to feel that same way. The next place I went where I had contact with strangers I made sure to genuinely compliment someone. I was reminded in a brief encounter at a coffee shop of the importance of building others up. That is a life lesson that I can use in just about any setting. We are surrounded by learning opportunities like that every single day, whether it's by copying someone else's positive behavior like I had or being reminded of how not to act by witnessing negative behaviors. Use those readily available moments to build your repertoire of skills because they will add to your personal growth. Your small sprinklings of joy upon others will not only make them a little happier, but it will also remind others to do the same.

Start building now:

Think of a recent and simple experience like my coffee shop one. Where were you/what was the setting?

Briefly recall what happened:

What lesson did you take away from the experience?

Was there anything "contagious" you could later apply in a different situation?

A sure way to find your best qualities is by pushing yourself to test your limits. You may just find that you have none. Some days I really believe I cannot handle any more because I am overwhelmed or defeated, so close to giving up and caving in. I am going through tougher times now than I ever have, as I continue an ongoing battle with MS, a divorce, a new and growing small business, and so many other things. It is okay to have those moments where you just feel overwhelmed, but trust me, you can handle it. You are limitless. The trick is to learn to go into any moment, task, or situation knowing it may be uncomfortable, challenging, or difficult, but that you can handle it. Those moments are just as necessary as the easy ones. Sometimes we must even put ourselves in uncomfortable situations knowing it will benefit our mission, it is the right thing to do, or it will lead to an overall greater good for all involved. No matter how uncomfortable it is, know you are capable. Pull knowledge from previous experiences and add to that knowledge and wisdom as you proceed through life. That wisdom will help your continued growth and ability to handle life's difficulties.

I have learned that pushing yourself to places you never thought you'd go is among the greatest treasures for personal growth. If it is challenging and even a bit scary, it is most likely worth it, in my opinion. You must realize that coasting along the same safe path you always have, even if you have experienced success along that very path, is a sure way to never grow or change. Even if you already knew the importance of challenging yourself, reminder is often needed because we, as humans, often become locked and comfortable in routine, which is not necessarily a good place to remain for long. Feeling content in life is safe and comfortable, but wouldn't you rather accomplish even more? Push your limits? Change the world?

Optimism, Selflessness, Respect. Hand in hand with personal growth comes the understanding of a need to tear down negativity in order to reveal and build yourself. Pessimism is like a sturdy brick wall: easy to build, nearly impossible to pass or break through, and a great barrier between two places. Well, the two places in this instance are the old you and the new you, and we have to always be moving in a positive direction with optimism, hope, and drive to continue unlocking potential on our path to success. If you have a giant brick wall of doubt and negative thoughts, you will remain in the same place forever until the wall is passable.

Being optimistic is very tough sometimes, but it is an understanding that things can be better, people can be good, and you can reach your goals. It's being flexible when things don't go as planned, finding positive use from not-so-positive moments, and never letting that small flame in your gut burn out. In this very moment you are learning how to find that potential within, and that tiny flame I am telling you to protect and keep alive is the heart of all potential you possess. What is that flame inside your soul? What does it represent? Continue considering what skills and knowledge you have, what tools you have, what potential you have to lead you closer to building your flame into a full-blown fire; that is when you will find your version of success. Believe!

What is your flame?

Write some thoughts on that little flame within. What is that thing you just cannot stop thinking about, that thing you are willing to work so hard to achieve? What is that interest or dream you want so badly?
Write your thoughts below:

Another imperative key to unlocking your potential is learning how to be selfless, even on a path to find your own success. To be completely honest, stepping on everyone around you to get where you want to be never ends well. Treating others poorly, lying, betraying others to build your own empire, or narrowing your focus to only benefit yourself will not bring you happiness or long term success. Those negativities typically come back to haunt later. A huge part of becoming a highly successful person is gaining respect from others while growing into a great leader, and neither of those are possible if you continuously push others down. Instead, try being a good person, strive to stay positive, and try to include others and help build others up along your journey. Think of it this way, you have many experiences, skills, and your own knowledge and usefulness. So does each other person, so you can take from them, learn from them, but only if you are kind and good. It is a steady balance. We can all help each other grow. You can still get where you want to be while helping others, and you will gain so many new friends and resourceful people along the journey if you take a route of selflessness to get to the top.

It is easy to get caught up in your own ambitions, so try to find ways to step out of that pocket and incorporate others. Meet new people as often as you can, help others if you can, show support for others who are trying to reach similar goals to yours, respect and seek guidance from people who already possess something you seek, and share your knowledge and skills. All of those people will remember what a kind, positive, driven, and good person you are, and it will inspire them to be the same. You may make new friends and will certainly gain useful resources by being kind and personable. Reaching goals isn't easy, and anytime you can network and build relationships with people it is a chance to create a sort of support team to help make your own journey easier and more rewarding.

Take a moment to think of and list someone (or multiple people) who is on your team and could provide useful skills, knowledge, and support to you and your journey to reach your goals.

Now, think of someone (or multiple people) who you do not personally know but could easily get in touch with who may be useful on your journey. How would getting to know this person better benefit you?

Gaining respect requires work on your part, but the process is a simple one:

- Show respect for others. Holding doors, supporting others' efforts, complimenting a job well done, whatever it is do it with respect.
- Show that you are serious and driven in your efforts, which means making conscious decisions, creating a transparent and accessible look into your intentions, and let people see you working your butt off to reach your goals
- Help others, don't just continuously ask for help. Providing for others and receiving from others is a balance, and you have to give without expecting anything in return.
- Take your time. Take time to learn as much as you can, build your skills, ask questions and practice, whatever you need to do to get to your goals you can gain respect along the way.

People are always watching, especially in today's world of social media. Gaining respect isn't about showboating all the good deeds you are doing, but rather allowing others to see the real you and all the work you are putting in, constantly inspiring using positive actions. You can tell people all day what a great person you are and about all the great things you are doing, but until they see the action for themselves, the respect will be guarded and hesitant. You can gain respect simply by being honest and real in all you do. It's okay to make mistakes, but learn and grow, and apologize if necessary! Just be real and truthful. Gaining respect and giving it are both vital to being happy and successful, so just go for it!

What does respect look like, sound like, feel like to you? Use the space below to write down your own definition and examples of what respect is.

Leadership Potential. Leadership, even if your goal isn't to be a 'person in charge' is key to unlocking your potential. You will read later two entire chapters on how to become a better leader and what that means, but the main thing is understanding the definition of leadership is much different than it was thirty or even ten years ago. Even if your goal is to be part of a team, what you will see is that the idea of a team means bringing together a group of leaders who all seek the same end-game and are able to work together to get each other there. So, even if you are thinking to yourself how badly you do not want to be a leader, fear not because leadership is something we all already possess a touch of, and you can and will get there. Now, let's work on unlocking that potential to move you closer to happiness and accomplishment.

Part 3

There is Value in That!

Which experiences are helpful? The answer to that question is: all experiences are. So many times we go through tough times and can unfortunately see only the bad surrounding us. I am guilty of allowing a sort of darkness to drape my mind during wicked experiences I have gone through, and it is not the ideal place to be. Speaking from personal experience and from observing others, we as humans sometimes put blinders up to the potential good that can come from any bad situation, and I honestly believe it is okay to allow yourself to fall into that moment of sorrow and defeat but only briefly. There is a sort of empowerment and motivation that accompanies the ability to pull yourself out of that momentary defeat and emerge stronger than before. We will get more into that, but start to repeat and remind yourself that there is value in bad experiences.

There is also worth from good things we go through, but you already knew that. Happy feelings, confidence, optimism, drive, are all things humans often feel when everything is happening in our favor or when something particularly good happens. We can learn so much from good experiences, and often gain great momentum from them. One of the most precious lessons to be learned from positive experiences may be how to pocket those moments and save some to pull out in the not-so-good times. Learn to appreciate every positive experience and moment and cherish those times as though they will be the last. Combining the hard times with the positives is what keeps us humble, so we must appreciate them all. I like to think of life's rollercoaster of ups and downs as challenges to keep us on our toes. Without both the ups and the downs our lives would be one boring, straight, monotonous path. Instead, our lives have the capability to be amazing journeys of learning, changing, overcoming, and more!

The important thing to take away from this lesson is that both good and bad experiences are inevitable in life, and both can be hurtful and helpful in our life progression. Those who gain wisdom from all experiences are true champions, and each and every one of us has the potential to do that, including you!

Good times and all they bring. I need to repeat this, as it is vital to understand in order to gain all you can from this: good experiences have almost as much potential as bad ones to create negativity in our lives. You have to learn how to cope and grow from every single experience, which means recognizing positives and negatives and how to use those to move forward in all situations. How could good experiences possibly cause any type of bad, you may ask? Think of a really happy moment in your life, a time when something went your way and brought you joy. It is simple to pinpoint every constructive thing about that situation. But think about this: the added pressure or stress that situation could have caused, the opportunity that situation had to create too much pride, the chance that joyful thing for you could have caused someone else sadness, or whether that joyful thing could have been stripped away from you. Those are just things to think about, potential negatives caused like a ripple effect from something jubilant. Think of this, you try out for a spot in a live theater role and get the part. The moment you learn you were chosen for the role you truly hoped for is a wonderful and joyful moment, but on the flip side someone else who wanted that role is having a particularly tough day learning he did not receive the role. Another example would be those times an athlete proves victorious in a game or match, yet the coach follows up the congratulations with a skill or moment in the game that the player or team could have improved. For example, a runner wins his race but still did not beat his own personal record. The moment he won the race was a wonderful one that he will always remember, but there is room for growth and improvement in that glorious moment. While that may not necessarily be a negative thing, it is still a small storm cloud hovering a good experience. There are always positives with negatives and negatives with positives. You must be able to prepare and recognize downfalls to good scenarios in order to maintain a general happiness. Don't get me wrong, you should absolutely revel in all the happiness that comes your way, even the small moments, but don't be afraid to share it and continue growing as a person from those moments.

Think of a good moment:

Think of a personal positive experience (big or small). Briefly describe the memory and what happened:

What is a <u>positive</u> lesson, skill, or useful tool you learned and took from that experience?

What was something (not necessarily negative) that needed improvement, was bad or negative, or could have been done differently or was an additional lesson learned from that experience?

Bad times generate progression. You may know this or you may have never experienced something soul crushing, but in life terrible things are sometimes thrust suddenly upon us. These heartbreaking circumstances are often capable of breaking a person to the point of numbness. It is not uncommon for those type of severe situations to break a person to the point that she no longer appears as the same person, maybe she cares less about things that used to be important or neglects things she used to take pride in. Whether you have been through something like that or not, it is important to understand what it takes to rise from it rather than allow it to consume your life. This type of wisdom is vital to traveling through life on the happy and successful course we are aiming to take. Like good experiences, bad ones can change a person, and the toughest thing is forcing those moments to change you for better rather than for worse. You just need to be able to find usefulness in even those terrible times. Survive the wrenching pain to find usefulness in order to create a tool that allows you to continue to grow and succeed. The skills to find practicality in every situation (good and bad) is so valuable, but it is tough and requires intention and thought.

The ability to use life's moments to your ability and growth as a person is key to finding true success and happiness. Imagine a life where anytime something good happens you only somewhat appreciate it and when something tragic occurs you let it tear you down completely. That is no life to live, a repetitive cycle, a carousel going nowhere except round and round. You have to learn how to think through instants and take away useful tools. Reflection and careful thought are often necessary to really shed the skin holding back your growth. I am now going to ask you to recall a tough time:

Briefly describe a time in your life that was challenging, difficult, or seemingly unsurpassable. What about that situation was negative, and how did it make you feel?

Now, this may be challenging, but think of the aftermath of that same experience. Recall one (or more) good or positive lesson or experience that came from the situation (even if it didn't come until some time after the experience was passed).

My life-changing moment and tools I gained from it. If you haven't been handling situations the way you believe you should be, or if you haven't experienced anything overly joyful or painful thus far, it is okay. You can still begin to shape and sharpen your ability to gain wisdom from experience. Likewise, if you have experienced overwhelming joy and positivity or continuous despair or struggle, you can also reflect on those or start shaping your ability to gain wisdom now. It is never too late to gain valuable skills.

Like most people, I have moments of life that brought sadness or defeat, and I have wonderful memories of great times that brought happiness into my life. I remember situations I did not handle well and ones I handled surprisingly well. For me, it took one major life-changing event to open my eyes to how inconsistent I was in taking advantage of the potential in each of those moments. I even wish I could repeat some past experiences in order to apply what I now know in them to create different outcomes or appreciate those moments more. I don't want it to take a huge life-changing moment for you to recognize missed opportunities or under-appreciated moments, but rather for you to have the knowledge, wisdom, and skills to conquer and gain strength if something like that ever comes along. If you already experienced one of those huge moments, regardless of how you handled it you can reflect on the situation and re-handle it in ways. Apply your new thoughts and knowledge to the situation and take away new wisdom from it. Even if the situation was far in the past, try to gain something new from it now. The memories from experiences are always with us making it possible to reflect on them whenever we want. In fact, oftentimes it takes a lengthy amount of time for a person to truly gain wisdom and knowledge from an experience because we continuously learn and grow, which changes our opinions and perspectives.

To be clear, I have had more than one negative experience in life, and I have had many blessed ones. One in particular, however, really opened my eyes and led to a wisdom and understanding of what it takes to truly arise from a situation. It made me and continues to make me wiser, stronger, and more capable of reaching my successes. Please remember, every experience's severity is situational, meaning my moment is no worse than the next person, but each person compares her experience to only her other experiences, thus creating a gauge of how serious any particular moment is. For me, this life-changing event was huge in a very negative way because, though I had already been though very tough times at that point in my life, this particular news was the one I believed was the worst. It created more fear, doubt and uncertainty, and sense of defeat than any experience I had ever had. It was something I had absolutely no control over, and I questioned whether I could make it through. I even had moments of absolute defeat and surrender. So what is it, you ask?

I have always been athletic with a passion for fitness and health. I work out and am active in different ways every single day. My friends and family have for years expressed their thoughts of my complete craziness because I wake up at 4a.m. to work out almost every day. I admit, it is a very early workout and I don't always feel like waking up that early to go to the gym. It is a habit of mine, though, and health and wellness is one of my passions. When I was a sixth grade English teacher in Henderson, KY I was attending a class at the YMCA close to the school every Monday, Wednesday, and Friday around 5:30a.m. each of those days before going to school. When I left teaching and started working in recruitment at a local college, I stayed in the routine of driving to Henderson, KY for that same class. The people in the class had become my friends (seriously the nicest, coolest, most supportive people ever!), and I liked the routine, so the drive across the bridge from Indiana to Kentucky was well worth it. It was 2014, and I had only been working at my new job for a few months. It was fall.

I woke up, as always, and drove to Henderson for my Monday morning workout. I had a funny feeling in my feet that morning like the feeling you get when you sit on your leg too long and it goes "to sleep" and feels tingly. It wasn't so noticeable, and I was still able to walk and workout, but it was irritating and got a little worse during my workout. I went about my day as normal and took the day off from working out on Tuesday. When I woke up on Wednesday to go to my workout the pesky tingling was still there and had spread into my hands. By the end of my work out on Wednesday the sensation in my hands and feet was worse and even started to slightly hurt like when you wake up in the middle of the night and your hand or arm is asleep and throbbing a bit, and the instructor and even my classmates had noticed something odd or different in my work out that day.

I took the day off Thursday from working out again. When I woke up Friday to go workout I tried to stand to get dressed and could barely do so. I still went to work out thinking it may help alleviate some of the sensation, instead I was unable to complete the workout. The numbness and pain were so bad I knew something was wrong. I took the day off work and made an appointment with a local urgent care physician. The doctor I saw ran some blood tests and found nothing wrong. I was and had always been very healthy, and that is all that showed in the tests. He was bewildered and suggested I see my family doctor, so I called to request an immediate appointment for later that day. I always saw the nurse practitioner at my family doctor. She was very knowledgeable and so friendly. She is who I saw that day, and she did everything she possibly could to solve the mystery of what was wrong with me. With the numbness and pain I even started to feel a little out of it, I mean like the type of fog that fills your head when you have a bad cold or bad allergies except I had neither of those. The nurse practitioner ran tests and had books upon books open trying so hard to figure it out. She did some vision and neurological tests with me, she did a basic physical, and when she just had some working theories but no real proof to support those theories, she called in the two practice doctors. They repeated some of the tests, and together those three spent so much time and attention on me I knew something must really be wrong, but I felt surprisingly safe and calm in their attentive care. I may have been a little naïve, as well, because everything had been going well and the thought of any serious medical issues was one I wasn't really willing to consider.

After several hours, I started to feel absolutely drained, and they had all agreed on a handful of possible theories, most of which were neurological. So, they put in a call to a trusted neurologist in the area and got me an appointment for the next day. The neurologist was young and fairly new, but he took his time and care in my initial exam and made me feel calm and comfortable. I had never been to a neurologist before. I had rarely even had to go to any doctor other than for typical flu or cold, so sitting in a neurologist's office, knowing they specialize in brain related diseases and injuries was very terrifying. Dr. R (we will call him) was phenomenal. He was honest and attentive. He did all the standard tests, he reviewed every symptom, he sought perspective from other neurologists in his office, and though we hadn't yet found a solution by the end of my visit, he was determined to solve the puzzle and get rid of the awful numbness.

I was sent for MRIs of the brain and spine and, while awaiting those results, I was sent to the infusion center to undergo five days of intense steroids to try to alleviate the numbness and pain. The steroid treatment ended up working splendidly in removing the numbness. And while I was still not back to 100%, I felt much better afterwards. I will say, the steroid treatment was a bit of a catastrophe in itself. I have never been a fan of shots or needles, and while inserting the IV port (after seven tries) the nurse busted a vein causing my entire arm to fill with blood and bruise. It was painful and I cried more than a grown adult should. Looking back, that moment was the very least of my concerns, but it was overly stressful considering everything else I was experiencing. Other than extreme fatigue and nausea, the steroid treatments worked well, and I was thankful. We still didn't know what had caused it and awaited the MRI results anxiously, hoping for some one time incident. My husband of the time and my mom were with me the entire time. We went back to see Dr. R when the results were in, and I knew something was wrong when he personally called to tell me I needed to come in to review the results. I remember having a breakdown on the phone, mostly because I assumed the results were bad otherwise he would tell me over the phone, but tried so hard to hide the fact that I was crying. One thing about me is that I don't like to show emotion in front of others. I have always been that way, wanting to show a strong and fearless front. I didn't even know what the results were in that moment, but whatever it was couldn't be good news. I tried to remain confident and sound unconcerned on the phone with my mom when I called to update her but remember crying so much when alone in my car after getting off the phone with her. I knew if I showed worry and sadness she would feel that way even more.

I went in to get the results, and waited so anxiously for what seemed like hours but was actually only fifteen or twenty minutes in the waiting room. I remember smiling and having casual conversation with my husband and my mom. Doing that helped keep me calm, and I hoped it help keep them from worrying too. What I found when I walked into the exam room, where Dr. R got right to the point with grace and clarity, was an MRI showing multiple lesions on my brain and spine. He confidently explained that it was almost surely Multiple Sclerosis, a disease with no known cause, therefore no test to confirm the disease and no cure. Believing that is indeed what it was, we proceeded with the next steps which are to be tested for anything else it could possibly be just to prove it was actually MS. Tons of blood work, more MRIs, and about a month later, on Halloween actually, I received another personal call from Dr. R who confirmed it was Multiple Sclerosis. He wanted me to come in to discuss what that meant and how to proceed.

The words that stick out in my mind from the entire whirlwind of events I went through are, "There is no cure." No cure. Scientists don't even know what causes MS making it much more difficult to create a cure. MS affects each victim differently, so doctors can't even really tell me exactly what to expect. The doctor did a fantastic job explaining everything, and he brought my husband and mom in to explain it to them as well. He spent extended time with us, answering all our questions and explaining potential treatments. I fully trusted his opinion, and once he gave me some treatment options, I decided on one almost immediately. Not wanting to wait any longer, I told him that day which treatment I wanted to try so that he could proceed with prescribing it for me. I would have to complete a series of blood tests and a lumbar puncture to be sure I could begin on that particular treatment. Just the thought of more needles and testing felt overwhelming. High intensity specialty drugs cannot be purchased at a local pharmacy or consumed without pre-testing and are required a long process to obtain.

Now, just to explain a little more, treatments for Multiple Sclerosis are strictly to help prevent new lesions from forming and to try to control symptoms as much as possible. Symptoms can be anything from brain fog, to numbness, to dizziness, forgetfulness, vision and hearing problems, to paralysis of the legs or mobility problems, anything controlled by the central nervous system. In my own words, MS is damage to the Myelin Sheath protecting the nerves in one's brain or spine, which causes a sort of misfiring between nerves and creates both temporary and permanent symptoms. It is irreversible, but the ultimate goal is to keep damage from spreading. Symptoms come and go randomly (very willy-nilly, in my words) making it difficult to predict. Treatments aren't cheap and can cost upwards of $70,000 in some cases. We didn't think about any of that in the moment. I chose a moderately aggressive pill treatment, and insisted on starting it instantly. I started the treatment immediately upon receiving it from my doctor. He explained the potentially harsh side effects and asked me to keep a sort of journal of side effects I experienced. After only a month and a half or so of taking the treatments I would go through another round of MRIs just to check progress. My doctor was thorough and made himself readily available to answer questions anytime, but I was still scared, understandably.

One day I was the healthiest, most athletic and fit person I knew, and the next I had an incurable disease that essentially can cause complete immobility and paralysis. It all happened so fast that I really had no time to truly let it break me down, but I was terrified. Having never experienced anything like it, I instantly took on an attitude that it would be okay and wouldn't get worse. I kept thinking, "There is no way it can get worse. I'm Gina, the fit and healthy one. I have too much left to do in life to be troubled with this. It will all be fine." Those who know me well know I keep a very positive attitude always, sometimes an unrealistic positivity. This was one of those times. I thought if I keep believing that nothing too terrible could happen to me it would be true. But I was wrong. The goal is for no new lesions, or damage to the myelin, anytime a MSer goes in for MRIs. I went in for my follow-up MRIs believing that since I had started treatment and was actually feeling somewhat back to normal, that everything would go on as before. Boom, I beat this thing and am moving on. Piece of cake. That was not the case, and Dr. R's office called to tell me my MRI showed new lesions. Three new lesions. More damage. My heart dropped, and in that moment I had my first serious breakdown. I had been on my way to work but turned around instantly to drive home. I called my husband and he left work immediately to be with me. I sobbed so much I had to have him contact my mom to tell her the news. There was no way I could tell her. I was so emotional it was difficult to speak, but it was especially challenging to stop the tears when I heard my mom's concerned voice. We sat on our familiar couch, in our familiar home, where everything had been normal and great such a short amount of time ago. I couldn't get any words out. I was up to thirteen various sized lesions in my brain and three on my spine, and if it had progressed that quickly in a few short months, I started to imagine I would be in a wheelchair or worse in no time. The emotional pain was crushing and I could see no light in that moment. Dr. R had me come back in to discuss the news, and that is what saved me. His calm and hopeful demeanor appeased me and gave me a shred of hope.

After my husband and I spoke at length with Dr. R, we decided together that I would proceed with the treatment and that the new lesions could have happened prior to me beginning the treatment. We decided to wait three months to do another round of MRIs, at which time if no changes had occurred I would remain on the treatment, and if they had we would come up with a new plan. Dr. R called my mom and step dad in to explain everything. I remember my mom telling someone else later that she had been devastated in that moment to hear of the new lesions but when she saw me in that office with my head held high, no tears, even smiling and laughing and confident in the plan, she knew it would be okay.

I made a decision with the help of my hopeful doctor and supportive family that this thing wasn't over. I allowed for a few moments of despair and for feelings of fear, and I allowed myself to cry and feel vulnerable. Then, I made a decision to move past those feelings. I am a competitive person, and I would not let this thing get the best of me. If I spent all of my time worrying, crying, and in fear I would be missing out on the many moments right in front of me. I reminded myself that I could wake up unable to walk, or unable to see or hear, or any number of the other possible symptoms, and I chose to spend my time challenging myself to accomplish the things I knew I wanted and needed to. I would fight my way through until I couldn't fight anymore. It has now been a few years, and I am continuing to fight. I have since been through other life-changing events which have caused my symptoms to worsen, but I continue to fight and learn from those experiences.

Now, the real purpose to sharing this story is to exemplify that I could easily use MS as an excuse to stop working out or to focus on the symptoms I experience daily and to give up, but I choose not to, and I want nothing more than to help others learn how to do that. Symptoms of MS worsen with stress, so step one for me was to make a plan and alleviate as much stress as possible. My job was one where I spent a good amount of time sitting and endured mental stress from a sort of hostile boss, so I knew I needed to find a new job. My co-workers were so supportive throughout the entire process and helped me every step of the way, making the entire process a little easier. I learned the importance of taking things step by step. Planning out how to handle my new diagnosis was much more easily managed by doing small amounts at a time and remaining calm and driven.

I needed a job allowing more flexibility in the time I spent sitting versus standing, a job where I could be as active or not as necessary. Those are very difficult to find, so I decided to move forward with trying to start my own business so that I could dictate my own hours, sit when needed, stand and move when needed, etc. Originally, I was going to open a clothing boutique, a plan I had crafted with the partnership of one of my dearest friends, but something didn't feel right about going from the education field to the fashion one. I love helping people, and selling clothing felt senseless and shallow. As I moved through the months following the start of MS treatment I realized how much medical debt was involved with all the testing and treatments. My mom started a fundraiser to help pay the medical bills, and it was through that I learned that my new endeavor, whatever it ended up being, needed to be one where I gave back to others. People I knew gave small amounts and large, and even people I didn't know, had never met, were giving and writing the most supportive and inspirational messages in my fundraising page online. I felt inspired, lifted, and driven to do the same for others that these supporters were doing for me. Their support guided me through my hardest moments. People were good, and I needed to be that too. In such a negative experience being good and doing good for others was what would save me, pull me through, keep hope ignited within me. Thus, the concept of a boutique that gives back with every single purchase was born, and that is where I am today. Something so positive was derived from something so terrible, a beautiful ability that I hope to share with others going through tough times. You too can produce something magnificent in the midst of devastation. It is completely up to you how to handle hardships.

No matter the obstacle, you have to open your eyes to each moment of the journey and learn from it, cultivate. Have a break down, feel defeated, but get back up and grow stronger and more determined from each knock down. This brings me back to the entire purpose of this chapter, which is that you must use every single experience whether good or bad, big or small to learn and grow. Being diagnosed with MS was the worst thing to happen to me at that time, and seeing the outpouring of support and positivity from others was the most inspirational thing to happen to me at that time. One highly negative experience created one highly positive one, and I learned from that to be attentive and reactive to each moment, to be grateful and humble. You don't have to experience something life-changing to begin your own journey of wisdom, happiness, and achievement. Instead, you can start now, use what you do have so that you are already on an upward path and are prepared should anything ever happen in the future that is life-changing. Really focus on the big picture, how that one experience fits into your life and into this world. Once you learn that one single moment, no matter how serious, does not dictate your entire past or future but is only your present, your capabilities will be endless. Likewise, always remember that even if the world-shaking event is happening to you it is likely affecting others in your life. Focusing only on the negativity will lead to despair, but open your eyes to the entire existence of the event and how it fits into your world (past, present, future and everyone affected or involved) to avoid sinking into the negatives. Opening our eyes and our minds to more than just how we are affected allows us broader range for growth and understanding.

Now, it is your turn. Maybe you haven't had anything severely life-changing occur in your time on Earth, or maybe you have had several of those, either way take a moment to reflect on your own experiences:

What is something you have gone through (positive or negative) that disrupted your life plan or created an obstacle to overcome?

What knowledge can you take away from that experience to help move your life in a positive direction (even if it was a negative experience)?

Look around. You will slowly begin to understand how to take away positive wisdom and knowledge from bad experiences, but that is not the only tool you need to help build your path to happiness. Every perspective can be useful in helping you grow and change. Observing others is a free and easy way to expand your own toolbox, and it requires little to no extra effort other than understanding and an open mind. You never have to agree with someone else's perspective on a topic, but it is so very useful to pay attention to others and educate yourself on other points of view. You don't have to agree, but can you understand that other point of view's thought process? Maybe there is a small part of someone else's perspective that you somewhat agree with, which is useful in expanding your own thinking. Observing others' reactions may even provide you with an example of how you don't want to act or be perceived. If you witness someone losing their temper, breaking completely down, or embarrassing themselves with a dramatic response to something you may learn that you don't want to react that way.

Likewise, we can feed off behaviors and attitudes of others. Like when that kid on the playground told you he didn't believe you would climb to the top of the geo dome (that big rounded playground delight with bars for climbing, like a web). You were afraid of heights, but his lack of belief in you (paired with his double dog dare) gave you just the right amount of courage to give it a try. Or when you severely twist your ankle during a cross country meet and the crowd cheers extra hard for you, and your teammates slow their own paces to help carry you across the finish line. You gain a certain swelling belief within yourself from those reactions. You are also awarded valuable lessons on behavior from those situations, from observing others' reactions and actions. A child who grows up in a household of parents losing their tempers over trivial things can learn to replicate those behaviors or to behave differently having disliked the way those behaviors caused him to feel. Observing others is vital to our own growth.

Think back to my negative experience with MS (or a **negative** experience of your own). Here are examples of opportunities for gainful perspective observations:

- How others involved reacted/handled the situation

  - In my case, this could be me observing how my husband or mom reacted to my MS diagnoses at different stages in the process. Did they break down or remain hopeful? Were they confident in the doctor and in the treatments and care I received? I have also chosen to observe those who try and use my MS as an excuse for me or to feel sorry, which, in my mind, is a very undesirable reaction though I know most people don't even realize they are doing that.

Observing others in the situation and comparing their actions, reactions, and feelings to your own can be helpful in figuring out how to both handle and how not to handle a situation. In my case, my family followed my positive lead, fed from it, and cycled positivity back into me, which helped me maintain a hint of hope and strength. That, however, isn't always the case. There are times when those closest to your situation present negative behaviors, making it more difficult for you to generate positivity, but recognizing their negative reactions and learning how to create your own positivity is the skill I need you to begin to understand and build. I know that I wholeheartedly dislike when family or friends mis-blame my MS for feelings or behaviors I experience or use my MS as an excuse when I don't even do that. It is frustrating. I am still more active, healthier, and accomplish more tasks in one day that most people I know, and I pride myself on that, so I know how terrible it feels when loved ones feel sorry for or make excuses for you, so I take that and remember not to do that to others. The skill of generating your own reaction and opinion in any given moment rather than blindly following those of the ones around you is a vital one.

- How did strangers or those not as closely involved act/react to the negative situation?

  - In my situation, friends and strangers reacted with hopeful and positive words, even knowing the situation was far from a good and positive one. I used their positivity to build my own hope and certainty in the unsure situation. But I also experienced some negativity from people who believed MS would be the end of me and from those who pretended to support and understand but continuously made my environment a stressful and negative one knowing its effects on me.

Have you ever seen someone lose their temper over something silly? I have watched people I care about lose their temper, generate negative attitudes from one small event, or overreact to something petty, as I am sure you have. Use their negative reactions to recognize and learn how to handle your own similar situations differently. You cannot necessarily convince those negative over reactors to change, but you can lead by example by using your observations of them and dislike of how they handle their own situations to improve your own. It can be a contagious cycle if others observe your more positive approach to handling things, thus generating empowerment and respect for you. Truly being yourself, reacting and handling situations as you honestly see fit, and having the courage to act or react differently when you feel it is the right thing to do are all sure signs of a wise person.

So, you see, your own growth from any situation is almost equally important as those of others around you, but you must be wise in recognizing and being observant in those moments. This information, and these skills will cycle back as pieces of the larger puzzle that is your own success.

Avoid Excuses. The purpose of this chapter is to help you realize the importance of using every situation life puts you in to your advantage. Once you understand how to use to your advantage both good and bad situations, as well as observations of how others handle various situations, you will be able to gain the wisdom and knowledge necessary to truly find yourself. Once you find yourself, you will be able to pinpoint the things that make you happy and will be able to access that happiness. So, when I say I want you to use each experience I mean I want you to use each as a positive tool, a motivation, and not as an excuse.

It is so easy to generate excuses in everyday life. When there is something we don't want to do, we could easily make an excuse to get out of it. When someone criticizes a job done, we could easily make an excuse to explain why the job wasn't done better. When we do something we know wasn't the right thing to do or could have been done differently to make it a more pleasurable experience for someone involved, we could easily make an excuse to take the blame off us and place it on some other circumstance. Making excuses, however, is easily the most cowardly thing to do. Wouldn't you rather correct the situation, gain respect because of your ability to admit wrong or "suck it up," so to speak? Wouldn't you rather learn a valuable lesson that can be applied in place of an excuse anytime? Yes, it may be easier to make an excuse in the moment than to do the work, admit a wrong, or admit you didn't do your best at something, but if you go just one step further and be honest you will feel better, go further, be better, and gain ongoing rewards from it. For example, I could easily use having MS as an excuse (almost daily) to get out of simple things like working out, or working, or volunteering at a local organization, or to explain why I am grumpy, but I don't. Now, if MS is truly the reason I cannot complete a task it is completely acceptable to make that known if necessary. I, personally, try not to express when symptoms of MS are holding me down unless it is going to interfere with a commitment I have made or directly affect someone else.

If you have a legitimate reason for something that needs to be known, by all means make it known, but in efforts to move you closer to lifelong joy, start to avoid making pointless excuses. Take responsibility and act with intention. Admit if you are wrong or have done something wrong that created some sort of issue or need for explanation. You will be respected so much more for admitting it and making it right than for lying. If you made a commitment to yourself or someone else (Go to the gym tomorrow. Eat a salad for lunch. Meet for dinner.) do everything you possibly can to keep that commitment and complete it to the best of your ability. Replacing excuses with accountability and truth feels so good and provides so much more value in the long run.

Can you think of a time you or someone else made an unnecessary excuse? What was it?

How could that situation been improved?

Forgiveness and Forgiveability. Going along with our goal of not using excuses to get out of things or in place of owning up to something, it is important to be forgiving and forgivable. It is tough to forgive some deeds, and it is tough to recover from deeds done. Remember, in every situation there is good and bad. If you were the "good" try to forgive the bad, and if you were the "bad" do whatever you can to make it right. If there is disagreement on who was at fault, try to listen with understanding to the other person involved. You may realize that you both were somewhat at fault and may be able to learn from the mistake or misunderstanding. The ability to forgive, learn, and grow, is a rare and cherished one, but you can do it. Try to avoid doing things that require someone to forgive you, but we all make mistakes, so being able to confess, apologize, and do your part to be forgiven is also a very treasured skill. Forgiveness is a respectful asset, and you will be one step closer to your personal success once you begin to master it. Even if the other party refuses to apologize, be the bigger person and do your part to make your wrongs right.

What is on your mind?

Do you have any thoughts on forgiveness? Use the space below to write down your thoughts. Is there someone you are having trouble forgiving? Is there something you have done that you long to be forgiven for? Or just write your general thoughts and opinions on forgiveness and its role in your own happiness in life:

Trust. Rarely easy, learning to trust yourself and others, especially after heartache, is completely necessary if you want true happiness. It is already difficult enough to trust others without adding personal anguish caused by broken trust to the mix. Deceit seems more common now than ever before. Credit card numbers and identities are being stolen daily. Internet hackers steal personal information all the time. A recent rise in general theft and robbery crimes creates a sense of uneasiness and distrust. Learning to cherish those moments that prove positive humanity still exists is a golden skill. Some people don't trust law enforcement, while others don't trust our government. Others do, and those opposing opinions often do not trust each other. Recognizing reasons not to trust others is easy, much simpler than seeing reasons why we should. Hit and run wrecks, abductions, human trafficking and forced labor, deceitful and unfair bosses and leaders, cheating spouses, and on and on are very real examples of broken trust. We see those almost daily making it almost natural and expected not to trust others.

In my 32 years on this earth I have experienced very serious deceit and broken trust. I have also been the one to break trust. I finally understand the true value in keeping a promise, whether big or small. I finally understand the importance of cherishing beyond everything the relationships I have with others, and keeping my word is among the most important in maintaining relationships of all kinds. You need to understand that giving and accepting trust is vital in your journey to grow. I know it isn't easy, and you need to know it is okay to feel apprehensive and unsure. You may certainly give your trust sparingly and with fragility, but you have to shake all the anger and past experiences with broken trust little by little. Not everyone will deceive you the way others have, and even those who have may be capable of change. Traveling through this journey with a scorned and hardened heart will absolutely get you nowhere. Learn to trust again. Will you get hurt or let down again? Unfortunately it is possible that you will, but it is necessary to move forward with an open mind and an open, even if guarded, heart. Each moment you overcome the heartache of broken trust you shed your skin and grow a little.

Was there a time you broke someone else's trust? Even if it was something as trivial as telling a friend's secret in middle school of the boy she was crushing on, or something much more serious, what was it?

How did it feel when the other person found out you had broken their trust?

What did you learn from that experience, as the trust-breaker, and do you continue to carry that lesson with you?

Now, on the opposition:

Think of a time when someone else broke your trust (no matter how serious the moment). Briefly recall the experience:

How did you feel when you found out your trust had been betrayed?

What steps can you take to move forward, forgive, and trust again?

Part 4

Your Inner Leader

Leadership + Success. So you may be wondering what the correlation is between leadership and success. I know many people (myself included) who never before had any interest in being a leader. I was always very shy and quiet, introverted, and preferred to work as part of a team or share my creativity individually. In the past, leaders were the loud sort of in your face type people who enjoyed telling others what to do, or were the intimidating ones. The leader was often assumed to be the oldest person in the group, the bossiest, or the one who held the highest salary. You will understand shortly how that type of leadership is a thing of the past, and the new style of leadership may be perfect for you. Either way, it is important to understand what it takes to be a respectable and effective leader in order to reach your successes, and fear not, it doesn't involve you becoming someone you are not, but uses all the best of who you are.

Let's start with a general definition of leadership. To me, leadership at its best is the ability to use knowledge, skills, and experiences to progress toward a goal, while providing guidance and instruction to others who will use their individual skills to assist you in attaining that goal. Working together, each person adds value to the efforts and the leader acts as a working member of the team. A good leader listens and observes, using that knowledge to manipulate and shape the group's tasks in a positive and useful way. It is an act, an action, and is as much the ability to learn and act as an equal part of the team as it is to lead others. A good leader recognizes when her team members excel in areas where she may not or hold knowledge that she doesn't. She can praise them and encourage them to use and share those things with everyone in order for the team to grow together.

Firecracker Leader. When you think of lighting a bottle rocket firework (or any kind of fireworks, actually) on Independence Day with your friends or family, what do you think of? What does a firework look like when it ignites? How does it make you feel? For me, fireworks make my heart race in a good way, like excitement or a swelling of pride. The excitement after they are lit and before they explode is a positive feeling to me. They are vibrant, exciting, and millions of people around the world join to watch them and share in those happy moments. Fireworks are a celebration and are celebrated, and they create togetherness. A crowd of Fourth of July fireworks viewers holds a variety of opinions, life styles, social statuses, and personalities, but in that moment all of those things are forgotten, and the crowd is one, and they are proud and supportive. A combination of all of those things is exactly what a firecracker leader is and is capable of doing with a team, and is the kind of leader you need to be.

Imagine a person who has the ability to, focusing on a goal or project he or she is passionate about, bring others who share that interest together while generating an excitement all while exuding that vibrancy and electricity that drives the group forward in a positive way. Every person in that group may share those traits and may be ecstatic leaders too, and that is perfectly okay. Each member will represent their own personality, their own opinions, their own ideas and thoughts, but a good leader can capitalize on those differences and generate a common mission that brings those differences together with enthusiasm and positivity. The point is that whatever your goals, your dreams, passions, your successes are, you will want and need others to help you along the way, and since they are helping you achieve your goals you will need to lead them. Good leadership skills are directly linked to accomplishing the tasks you desire to accomplish, so why not become a firecracker leader to generate maximum results? You have leadership skills built into you, I promise you that, so all you have to do is build on what you already possess and continue to grow and perfect your bundle of leadership skills. You want to be sure everything you are working toward in life meets your dreams and expectations, so being the best version of yourself, the best leader possible will only add to the success of those goals.

Still unsure of whether you are cut out to lead others? Or maybe you believe you are already a highly effective leader, and you may very well be. Fear not, there are many leadership styles and types, and you can always become a better one. In the next chapter, you will work to try and discover which leadership style suits you best and will best work for you as you journey through life toward your dreams.

Team of Captains. I mentioned before how today's concept of leadership is much different than those of the past. If you think about groups, teams, community projects, or other situations that require a group of people to work together, you will begin to see what I mean. In the past, a project would consist of a leader (or boss, or captain) who told everyone else in the group what to do and had the final say in decisions. That leader often had a specific method the group should follow to arrive at a solution, regardless of their individual skills and opinions. Everyone else in the group would work on individual tasks assigned to them then come together for an end result. Some aspects of that method worked well. For example, each individual team member may have been assigned tasks fitting their specific skills or strengths, so the end result was a strong one having each aspect of it completed by those most fit to do so. There were some downfalls with that method as well. Some leaders may not be as great at leadership as they believed (and this is still sometimes the case), yet still proceeded to take complete control neglecting additional ideas from team members and putting on blinders to issues or changes needing made. Sometimes team members didn't pull their weight, or pulled too much weight. These issues still exist, obviously, but the new style of teamwork and leadership helps eliminate some of them.

So here it is, the new style of leadership. Remember, there are several types of leadership, but this visual will allow you to understand the basic concept of what it means to work with others or lead a group.

Team Leader
This person is responsible for guiding other team members in order to keep tasks on track. And meet deadlines. Takes on tasks just like other team members. Should listen and observe in order to best plan, manipulate, and progress the team's process, in a positive method, to reach goals.

Team Member	**Team Member**	**Team Member**
Also an effective leader. Uses specific skills and expertise to add to team's task. Is allowed to have a voice, ideas, and add creativity. Is praised and appreciated.	Also an effective leader. Uses specific skills and expertise to add to team's task. Is allowed to have a voice, ideas, and add creativity. Is praised and appreciated.	Also an effective leader. Uses specific skills and expertise to add to team's task. Is allowed to have a voice, ideas, and add creativity. Is praised and appreciated.

So you see, the new age concept of leadership is really not all that complicated. It is actually much like the old system in that it is a leader and a team of workers, but you will notice that each team member is encouraged to be his own style of leader within the group rather than just someone taking orders. Members are praised and appreciated for their individual skills and ideas. You will also notice that the leader acts as an equal member of the team and is encouraged to learn from the other members, sometimes just as much as they learn from her. The leader should work equally as hard as, and even harder than the other team members.

If you are the boss of a department of employees, as the person in charge you would guide them, give them constructive feedback on how to improve, praise their jobs well done, and learn from them. You have to understand that each and every player on a team is equally valuable, and the leader is a player on that team. As the person in "control" you not only have to act as an equal member of the team, but you also must manage and maintain the meeting of deadlines, positive team moral, act as the glue that holds the group together, and ultimately make sure the team gets from point A to point B to the best of its ability.

Remember, we are working toward getting you to where you want to be in life, whether you are focusing on a career path, overcoming life's obstacles, making a dream a reality, or just bettering yourself or finding happiness. Other people will be involved in your journey, it's inevitable, so you should discover what your best leadership style is and start building those skills so that your support team is fully equipped and highly effective when it matters most.

Take Control. Whether you are an adult who is unhappy in your current job or career, a high school or college student working to discover what you want to do with your life, or someone going through an insanely tough time in life, whatever your status right now in life, you can take or regain control. You can find happiness. Becoming an effective leader does just that, it allows you to have control of your life. There are always circumstances beyond your control, of course, but confidently taking control of your life can help you push through even those uncontrollable moments. Your team of supporters will help you reach your goals, but you have to be the most effective leader you can possibly be in order to do so. So, before you skip over this chapter afraid to step into a leadership role, or believing you are already the best leader you can be, stick with me and remember we can all always improve and grow, and remember we are working toward shedding fear to accomplish big things. You can do this!

I want to provide you with an example of how leadership is vital to every single person so that you can start to discover the usefulness gaining these skills has to you.

Example:

Situation

You are a college student. You aren't 100% sure your course of study is taking you to your dream job, but you are almost finished with school and unsure of what else you would do, so you stick with it. You know that you have always loved helping people, and will be able to do that with your degree once you graduate, but you just aren't sure the jobs associated with that degree will truly make you happy.

Small Step in the right direction

You love art, but you know that opening an art studio as your full time career is not realistically an option yet. So, you love helping others and you want to do that using your passion for art. What do you do? Take a small step in the right direction, and start a club or small organization, or create a website that focuses on using art to help others. Maybe you sell art online and give a portion of the proceeds to a cause you care about. Or you reach out to others interested in art or giving back and do a monthly activity or community service that involves art and/or giving back.

Focusing on smaller tasks like these will get your foot in the door and help you begin gaining valuable experience, skills, and steps in the right direction. So many times we are forced to put our dreams aside because of financial reasons. Starting a business of any kind requires money. Many hobbies we wish to make into careers aren't as financially rewarding as we need them to be. That is a fact, but that doesn't mean it is impossible, and it certainly doesn't mean a dream should be completely forgotten because of one set back. So, you decide to start volunteering once a month with handicapped kids by doing art with them. You would begin gaining experience and skills, but more importantly you would be networking, getting your name and intentions out to others, and you would be able to slowly build upon that to create something amazing. Will you have to work at that job your degree is getting for a while before you finally reach your ultimate goal of owning an art studio that gives back? Probably, but you will be so much happier already knowing you are moving in the right direction. Hard work truly pays off. I can tell you from experience that sometimes reaching for that dream of yours means working significantly harder at it than you would otherwise have to, but it is worth it.

How Leadership skills will play a role. When you start selling art online, you may not necessarily need help from anyone else, but it is always useful to accept help when possible. Reach out to other people you may know who have sold online or who are great with sales. Reach out to people who work for charity organizations to find out more about how you can use your new art project to help others. Though it may start with sporadic aid from others, when you finally reach your dream of opening your own give-back art studio, you will have collectively sought help from many people and will continue to more and more. Those people are helping you reach your goal, therefore you must take on a strong leadership role in order to successfully utilize their help and grow in the right direction.

The point is, even if you are taking on your beginning task alone you will inevitably receive help from others and be required to work with others. I own a small business where I currently employ no one but myself. Yet, many people participated in the process of opening the store, and I continuously work with others to grow the business. Since the store is my dream, my responsibility, it is up to me to act as the leader in all things involved with the store. I can use that leadership to learn from others, gain valuable skills, meet goals, guide others who are helping so they are clear on tasks needed of them, etcetera. It is vital for you to build your leadership skills and to be a good one; be kind, fair, and always learn and grow. Leadership skills are parallel with success, and we are never done growing as leaders.

Leadership + Respect. You are never too young or too old to gain respect and give it. Likewise, you must give respect to get it. Have you ever had a boss or team leader that is that stereotypical "bad" leader who all the team members or employees dislike and talk negatively about regularly? I have had several managers, team leaders, or bosses in my time who fit that description, and I never quite understood why they acted that way. It is a rather simple concept, good leadership and respect, that is. You give respect, you are a fair and kind leader who is always willing to learn from team members and appreciate their work, you gain respect. Will you please everyone? Most likely not. Because of the wide range of opinions and personalities that exist among humans, it is nearly impossible to please every single one. If you give respect and stay humble through your journey to reach your goals, you will slowly gain respect and build a reputation as a solid leader who can be trusted. People want to improve, so by guiding them and aiding them with their own growth while showing them you too are growing generates mutual respect. That is exactly what you want, no matter your goals. Being a good human, trustworthy and trusting, fair, and kind will begin growing your respect.

I've told you some of my thoughts on what a good leader is, but now it's your turn. Think about leaders you have worked with or known. Think about what they did well and what they could have done better to be a more effective leader. Then, determine what your concept of a good leader is.

Think of a leader you have known. What was he/she the leader of?

What did this person do well in the leadership role?

What could have made this person a more effective leader?

What do you believe makes a phenomenal leader? Write your thoughts here:

Some people have severe misconceptions about what a boss, leader, or captain, is. I want to be sure you have a positive understanding of what it takes to be a good leader and understand that you are fully capable of doing so. You already know a leader should be expected to be the ultimate team player and should always learn from and work with the team or group, rather than merely bark orders to them or expect them to do all the work. Another huge misconception about leadership is that the leader is whoever is oldest or makes the most money. Again, that is an old fashioned concept. Have you ever heard the term "Fair-Trade?" Fair-Trade organizations are nonprofit businesses that employ artisans (usually in developing communities) who provide services or craft items to be sold. When those items are sold, the majority of the profits go right back to the individuals who made them. This method gives the employees, the team members, fair wages for the work they are doing rather than providing an aggressive amount to a CEO or business owner and very little for the employees. The leader is also paid fairly and has the job of working, hands on, with the team and guiding and instructing them. So, you see a leader is not determined by who makes the most money. In a fair-trade setting the leader may make the same or barely more than the team members based on what work is being done. I want you to strive to be a Fair-Trade style leader. Leaders are not determined by who makes the most money, who yells the loudest, or who is the oldest in the group. It may seem obvious, but the leader is just that, the person motivating and leading the others. It's so simple. Let go of needing all power and superiority and learn to appreciate the individual skills, ideas, and work of each member of your team. Below is a simple list of expired concepts of leadership vs. the type of leader I want you to become in order to take charge of your own life and responsibilities. Pair your newfound leadership skills with your own personality and leadership style, which you will discover in the next chapter, and you are sure to excel at anything you set your mind to!

Do (Firecracker Leader)	**Don't (Old-fashioned leader)**
• Encourage brainstorming among team	• *Don't* provide all information and snuff brainstorming from others
• Share information to keep all team members in the loop	• *Don't* hide information/keep information all for yourself
• Show appreciation and praise to team members	• *Don't* ignore jobs well done, ideas from others, or discourage team participation
• Provide a clear team goal or task	
• Assign jobs to yourself and your team members	• *Don't* confuse team members by providing vague goals or instructions or by changing them frequently
• Provide constructive feedback	
• Solve problems and issues with a level head and by getting to the base of the problem.	• *Don't* bark orders and give yourself none or give orders without specifics
• Be flexible and willing to adapt and change even if it was someone else's idea	• *Don't* insult team members or intentionally humiliate them
• Remain humble and admit wrongs	• *Don't* lose your temper or "solve" issues by yelling or insulting
• Remain positive, enthusiastic, and optimistic	• *Don't* refuse to change or adapt or discourage new ideas
	• *Don't* make excuses or blame others for mistakes, failures, or issues
	• *Don't* be negative, pessimistic or doubtful, or power-hungry

Remaining humble and kind is a good place to start as the leader of your group. The person next to you will always know something you do not or possess a useful skill that you do not: learn from them! Even history's best leaders had flaws. It is a good thing to continuously learn and develop as a leader. People feed on others' energy and attitude, so present positivity and enthusiasm to set the tone, and don't be afraid to feed off your team members' throughout the journey.

I remember in teacher workshops always being told that a leader is not necessarily a boss, and that is a sort of valuable concept I would like you to adopt. Being a leader doesn't mean being bossy. Rather, it is almost even more important as a leader to close your mouth and open your ears. Listening to your team members and actively observing will allow you to bend and shape, manipulate the process in a positive and effective way. Your assignments and communications with team members should be filled with intention to maximize results, which requires awareness of details that can only be observed through listening. It is up to you to keep things running smoothly with your team while allowing them to work at full potential. Think of the type of leader you respect and enjoy working with. Be that!

Now you will begin determining and understanding how you can best use your new concept of leadership in your journey to succeed. Your role as the leader may change throughout different moments in your voyage.

Consider any leadership experience you have. Jot down some ways you would like to improve your leadership skills, how you plan to do that, and any other thoughts you could come back to throughout the process.

How can you implement positive traits of a leader in your current life?

Thinking ahead to potential next steps in life, how do you foresee yourself utilizing firecracker, positive leadership skills?

How do you foresee yourself growing as a leader in your efforts to reach your goals?

Part 5

Leadership Types

Where do you fit in? Leaders come in a variety of forms, but the truth is that anyone can take on that role if they possess enough care, passion, and drive and are able to act selflessly and with intention. To begin building your leadership potential, take these steps:

1. Find your passion(s), that thing that truly ignites your fire and creates joy for you.
2. Desire to share that passion with others.
3. Use your knowledge of effective leadership to begin shaping and establishing yourself as a leader

You already know that taking charge and accepting help from others (putting you in that leadership role) is vital to your progression toward happiness and success. Now you need to discover what style of leadership comes most naturally for you so that the process of becoming the best leader possible is a much easier one for you.

*Below you will find a list of what leadership potentially looks like. Circle or mark the ones that best represent you and your natural personality. *It is expected that no person will match with each of the below. Just be honest, and circle the styles that come naturally to you.*

1. Teaching others a skill you enjoy.
2. Helping others or a team reach a shared goal/accomplish a task.
3. Help organize or plan something like an event, fundraiser, etc. that will require teamwork to accomplish.
4. Ability to give clear directions and alter those directions to fit the understanding of team members.
5. Ability to listen to needs, concerns, and ideas of those you work with.
6. Learn how to build on ideas, add creativity and insight to take ideas to a new level.
7. Using others' ideas and plan concepts to help create forward progress from them.
8. An ability to pinpoint strengths and weaknesses in others and use that to assist them in personal growth.
9. Appreciation for perspectives and opinions
10. Ability to allow others on your team to take the lead when their skills or abilities supersede your own in a particular area for the overall betterment of the group and its task. Ability to collaborate and take instruction from other team players.
11. Ability to problem solve and assist others in doing so
12. Ability to reach the root of issues in order to maintain forward progression and focus
13. Ability to praise and uplift others without jealousy or envy
14. Able to recognize and focus on the "big picture" in order to reach the goal
15. Able to make decisions with the ultimate goal in mind
16. Willing or interested in learning from others
17. Honest, trustworthy, trusting, able to admit wrongs
18. Respectful, mannerly, professional

19. Organized and able to delegate tasks for maximum results
20. Willing to take risks and create and share vision

The likelihood that you circled every single example of leadership as one you are superior at is slim. No single one of us can excel naturally at every single aspect of leadership. That is why it takes experience and practice, understanding, and time to build upon those skills we have less interest in or natural ability with. Once you are able to pinpoint the skills you naturally excel at, you can spend the majority of your time building upon the areas in need. Remember, like any other skill you try to improve, becoming a great leader does not happen overnight. So, even if you haven't yet decided your next steps toward your life goals it is never too soon to start building these skills. Find opportunities to work with others as a member of a team or initiate your own need to gather a group (like the art student example) to begin practicing working with others and building those skills. Joining local clubs or community groups is a great way to begin observing and practicing leadership skills while networking with others. There are often non-profit groups or clubs, or even leadership-specific groups you can join. Volunteering regularly with a local non-profit is another great way to network and learn valuable leadership skills. I like to suggest seeking volunteer opportunities relevant to your life goals so that you are also able to gain knowledge pertaining to your specific needs. Most importantly, be yourself. Use what you have, let your positive traits shine, and grow into the best version of yourself you can possibly be.

Now you can decide your most natural and comfortable leadership style (use the circled leadership skills from above) and focus on practicing and growing as that leader in your everyday life!

Various Leadership Traits and Styles. Read through the brief descriptions and examples of types of leaders below (this builds on the brief list from above). Note the ones that match how you typically choose to interact with others to complete tasks. The choices most natural and comfortable for you are the ones I want you to focus on using and building upon. You can then start to sprinkle in bits and pieces from other styles you are less comfortable with as you journey forward. You will notice that each style is then followed by an opposite style. You may be more than one, in fact, you may match with one from each pair! That is totally fine, and I want you to dig deep, be honest with yourself, and really start to explore every inch of your personal leadership style. Feel free to circle, make notes, and really own your styles!

The Outgoing Leader

This person prefers to be noticed and maybe even be the center of attention. He has no problem talking to people and is loud and confident. They may sometimes appear or seem bossy or overpowering, but they are great at demanding attention, giving direction, and accomplishing tasks. The outgoing leader may sometimes need to make intentional effort to avoid overpowering other group members (things like cutting others off when they are speaking, or completely overpowering a meeting). The enthusiasm is fantastic, but it should be reined in at times in order for team member to equally contribute.

If this is you, consider the following:

- Be sure to allow your team members opportunities to express themselves, even if they are quiet or shy.
- Be sure to continue learning from and listening to the opinions, ideas, and thoughts of your team members, even if they differ from your own.
- Use your ability to be noticed and take control to positively motivate and drive your team
- Use your ability to gain attention from others to present clear instructions and directions to move your team's progress steadily forward
- Remember you can always learn from those you are working with, even if they are introverted and shy.
- Lead with intent in a way that doesn't intimidate your team. Your outgoing personality may come off as intimidating to

those on your team who aren't quite as outwardly energetic. Intentionally create moments to show you are kind, appreciative, and open to their ideas.

Is this you? What are your thoughts on the reminders list? How can you use these suggestions currently? Write your thoughts below:

The Shy/Introverted Leader

Sometimes we think of the leaders of any group as the loudest one, the one barking orders, but leaders can be quiet and introverted people too. The shy or introverted leader prefers listening to others and will often take information in and process it internally before vocalizing a response. They will have no problem instructing the team and individuals on tasks and goals, but won't be as boisterous as the outgoing person when doing so. They have no problem with team members vocalizing and taking the lead on various aspects of a task, but maintain a steady, calm, and shared handle on tasks. This leader may have to intentionally speak louder or use intentional assertiveness to assure the team of his confidence and stability as a leader.

If this is you, consider the following:

- Since you are quiet and calm, you must intentionally express your excitement and positivity to help generate a positive energy within the group.
- You will need to begin to feel comfortable keeping the group on task should they get off task or distracted. This may require you to speak up or create your own methods of demanding attention. It is okay to designate a more outgoing person who you trust as the person "in charge" of helping drive focus.
- Consider communicating more one on one with individuals on your team, as it may be more comfortable to you than entire group discussions and meetings. While you may have to have group meetings occasionally, it is perfectly acceptable to meet one on one with team members to discuss their tasks, goals, progress, etc.
- Use your fine ability to listen to gain and share knowledge.
- Consider using a written guide or checklist to help keep team members on task rather than vocalizing those things.

Gina M. Mullis

- Use body language and eye contact to demand attention rather than a loud, booming voice.
- You may be quiet, but you are intelligent and strong. Be sure to express, (in writing, in a video to team members, in the group setting, or one-on-one with team members) your specific intentions, passion, energy, and knowledge to your team.

Is this you? What are your thoughts on the reminders list? How can you use these suggestions currently? Write your thoughts below:

The Teacher Leader

This person, whether a literal teacher or not, truly enjoys educating others in some capacity. They may sometimes come off as a "know it all," but really just enjoy sharing what they know with others. They have a knack for using details and clearly describing expectations, tasks, and concepts. They are able to manage others well, multi-task, and provide positive feedback and constructive criticism. They typically enjoy collaborating on projects.

If this is you, consider the following:

- Use your ability to instruct to your advantage by providing clear and detailed goals, tasks, and intentions to team members.
- Intentionally step back in order to allow team members to step into the spotlight sometimes. This may be difficult since you love being the instructor, but the best part about teaching is learning!
- Lead by example by helping your team members become better teachers/leaders themselves by showing them a positive style of teaching. Show them how to effectively collaborate.
- Use your ability to instruct to reward your team members for jobs well done
- Generate group discussions and guide them, but be sure not to take over discussions. Share the stage by acting as a mediator for team members and add your voice occasionally.
- You are a teacher, which is a great natural leader. Use that to produce a productive team capable of accomplishing any goal.
- Use constructive criticism to help group members improve and grow. Likewise, accept constructive criticism from group members to improve yourself.

Gina M. Mullis

Is this you? What are your thoughts on the reminders list? How can you use these suggestions currently? Write your thoughts below:

The Learner Leader

This person enjoys learning and is perfectly capable of teaching but thoroughly loves learning from others. They are typically good and attentive listeners and are able to generate new concepts and ideas from material learned. The learner leader typically enjoys allowing team members to step up into leadership roles within the group to provide perspective and new ideas, but is also capable of taking the lead to maintain order. This person is one who typically has multiple ideas soaring and may have to use intention in organizing those ideas and remaining on task with one idea or project at a time.

If this is you, consider the following:

- Be sure to provide clear process and intentions for group members before encouraging them to take the lead. There should be a clear and consistent process in place to maintain order.
- You may consider meeting with team members individually to understand their ideas, thoughts, progress, and more then report your findings to the group in group discussion.
- Be sure to clearly define what you expect of each group member and express the goals and intentions clearly, even if you want each team member to step into leadership roles throughout the process.
- You are responsible for setting the standards for how the group will operate. Be sure not to skip that step!
- Do what you can to stay organized and focused on the goals at hand.

Is this you? What are your thoughts on the reminders list? How can you use these suggestions currently? Write your thoughts below:

The Organized/Detailed Leader

This leader is very detail oriented and organized. They like to plan each team member's role, tasks, and goals and orchestrate the entire process. They need to outline meetings and tasks, and expect everyone involved to stick to that plan. This leader is great at meeting deadlines and keeping everyone on task. They may have to use intention to prevent themselves from micromanaging too much.

If this is you, consider the following:

- Your ability to plan and organize is very useful in the process of reaching your goals, but remember the road map concept. Your plans will not always remain intact or be followed exactly, and you must be able to adapt with flexibility to continue toward the goal.
- Be attentive to your team members and their personal styles of accomplishing tasks. Some people don't accomplish tasks as well with too detailed of a plan, so it may create difficulty or frustration for those people. Be open to providing your blueprint and allowing team members to follow it as needed in order to reach the intended goal.
- Help others stick with your level of organization by providing interactive check lists, calendars, or other organizational tools to help your team follow your expectations.
- Be sure to communicate clearly and often your goals and expectations of each team player.
- Relax and try your best to remain flexible to changes.
- If there is a specific way you'd like your team members to stay organized be sure to communicate that with them. Again, not everyone organizes tasks the same as you, so don't assume they will.

Gina M. Mullis

Is this you? What are your thoughts on the reminders list? How can you use these suggestions currently?

The Creative Leader

The creative leader is full of ideas with eccentric excitement and energy. Their minds often race ahead of their physical capability to accomplish tasks, so they tend to hop from one task to another or from one thought to another, which can be confusing for team members. They are typically fun and have colorful and creative ideas and love hearing creative ideas from their peers. They are typically positive leaders with contagious energy and passion, but sometimes have trouble organizing a clear path.

If this is you, consider the following:

- Your energy is perfect for a leadership role, so be sure to use that to motivate your team
- Take time before meeting with team members to construct a clear outline or guide for each team member that shows your goals, intentions, and expectations. It may even provide specific tasks for each team member. This will also help you remain on task.
- Try to focus and follow your outline when communicating with your team members. Some of them may have a more organized style of thinking, so your million mile a minute mind may create frustration and confusion to them! We don't want that, so be attentive to the needs of your team. You want everyone on the same page.
- You come up with ideas quickly and sometimes while in the middle of a different thought. Try keeping a small journal on hand at all times to jot down interrupting thoughts rather than expressing them as they come. This will help you stay focused on one task at a time, helping you stay on task and progressing forward toward your goals.

- Try to accomplish one task at a time, and encourage your team members to try and do the same. This will help maintain organization and order.
- Try meeting one on one with team members periodically to make focusing on specific tasks, concerns, thoughts and ideas, and efforts easier for you. One at a time is easier for creative people than a group setting with ideas flying!

Is this you? What are your thoughts on the reminders list? How can you use these suggestions currently?

No matter what kind of leader you are, be a good one. A good leader goes beneath the surface, listens to others, learns, cares, observes, grows, and continuously adds layers to their souls and to others'. It is no secret that helping others makes us feel good, and in this scenario they are helping you reach your goals. You may be the leader, but your team is there for you. They are supporting you and giving you their time, attention, and energy. That is a huge deal! It is the least you can do to respect their voices and be the very best leader you can be throughout your journey to success.

You are already doing a fantastic job of pinpointing which leadership skills you possess and what leadership styles best fit your natural ability. Now, I challenge you to begin really focusing on the following: (feel free to jot down ideas as you go!)

Discover what leadership skills you already possess.

What kind of leader can you see yourself as or want to be?

How could you use your existing knowledge and skills to help others?

How can your personal adversities and obstacles benefit and motivate you as a leader?

Think of situations where you were fearless and confident and focus on applying that to your leadership.

Combine your definition of success with your goals and intentions, and add in your clear style of leadership to begin creating an effective and sturdy plan of action. You have to know yourself and start generating steps to take toward your goals that are natural and not forced. Remember we are always learning and changing, and our goals and leadership styles grow and change with us, and that is okay! Let's end this chapter by writing down some thoughts on how you can use your personalized leadership style to begin growing as a person and start taking your goals and happiness to the next level!

After working through this chapter and understanding various aspects of leadership, what leadership traits and styles did you find best suite you?

How can you start to implement your leadership skills in your life now?

What aspects of your leadership personality can you start to build and improve and how can you do that?

Part 6

Be Respectful & Be Respected

R.E.S.P.E.C.T. If you haven't yet realized, all aspects of respect, leadership, knowing yourself fully, honesty, trust, positivity, drive, and motivation are vital in generating happiness for yourself. All of those things can pull you through those life-changing experiences. All of those things can create true happiness for you. All of those things can lead you to your own personal success. They are all vital, working hand in hand to grow you, so it is important to fertilize each.

You have already begun discovering the leadership potential in you and understanding how that fits into your aspirations. Now, you will take yourself to the next level, up the next steps, toward building your life, your dream, your success. It's time for that big change, and you are on your way! As you grow your leadership skills and continue to find, harness, and shape your passion and path you will begin gaining respect in a variety of ways. Likewise, giving respect long before that is important. Were you raised to believe that a company's custodian or maintenance staff deserve the same treatment and respect as that company's CEO? If not, start believing it now! It is insanely true and that mind set is the only way you will ever fully open yourself to giving and receiving ultimate respect. A job title does not define us, but our treatment of others sure does. You must remember that each and every human being is blessed with her own individual set of skills, has her own definition of success, and has her own style of leadership within. So, drop any judgements and begin giving respect to all people. A happy and successful person is a good person who is observant of others no matter social status. Listen, learn, and grow from what you see and hear, and you will likewise gain the respect you deserve.

The concept of respect is one we all learn early in life. Our kindergarten teachers educate us on the golden rule of treating others how we would like to be treated, but as we age we are sometimes blinded by ambitions, calloused by hardships and wrongdoings, or shaped and influenced by negativity that creates blinders to that golden rule. If that is you, make conscious efforts to strip away those blinders to return to the simple understanding that you need to treat others how you wish to be treated. This concept can also circle back to your efforts to stop making excuses. Drop excuses and take ownership for how you treat others. While I was always taught to treat others with respect, I have realized through my MS diagnosis and through the first two years of owning Amerie Boutique that giving respect is vital. You never know what struggles are presenting themselves in another's life, and while I am not asking you to allow others to "walk all over you," so to speak, I am merely asking you to always present a fair respectful attitude. How a person acts toward others is beyond your control, but how you act is not.

Their reaction toward others is beyond your control, but how you act is not. I wanted to express that statement again because of its importance. Do your part and try not to stress over someone else's disrespect. We can lead by example and try to educate and show others what respect looks like, but it is up to them to make those changes within themselves. When I was a teacher and now as a business owner I experience unnecessary disrespect from others occasionally. I used to allow it to anger me, and I would try to point out their disrespect, which would only make them behave using even more disrespect. When I finally realized those people cannot change until they realize they need a change, a weight of anger and frustration was lifted. It is still frustrating when people are disrespectful for no reason, but all we can do is our part to exemplify respectful behavior in hopes that those disrespectful people adopt similar behaviors and make a change.

So, how do you begin gaining respect right now? Start focusing on using positive intention with others:

- Learn patience (I know, this can be tough!)
- Learn understanding
- Have an open mind: listen to others' opinions even if you disagree
- Learn to compromise with others
- Develop better communication skills (it doesn't hurt to build written and vocal skills)
- Learn to compliment others (and mean it!)
- Be humble, and stay that way no matter how successful you become!
- Handle bad situations with grace and pull positivity from them
- Remain positive through hardship
- Continue developing your skills and crafts
- Find compassion in moments, kind words you hear, and actions you witness
- Focus on accepting others' opinions even if you disagree, and try finding value in their points of view.
- Gain respect by working hard and treating others well and not by trying too hard or forcing others to see your good deeds.
- Note behaviors of those around you who are highly respected and learn from them!

That was a long list. I want you to read it one more time, and circle three or four items you want to start working on today. You never have to try to accomplish all you are learning through this program all at once. It is a process and is most effective if you take time to focus on each little part at your own pace. All of the actions, reactions, and ways of living in that list are traits of a good person on her way to becoming a successful and happy person. Couple those with strong determination, drive, and other empowering leadership skills, and you have what it takes to be successful and truly happy, able to conquer anything!

I like to think of respect as something simple and small that makes a huge impact. Like a beautiful butterfly, gentle and small in size these creatures make a huge impact on nature by acting as vital pollinators. They are often overlooked, and they are not thought of as a force to be feared, but should they ever go extinct the planet would suffer fatal devastation. Being respectful is very similar. Something as small and gentle as a kind word, holding a door for someone, politeness, of a genuine listening ear could generate monumental thoughts, feelings, or actions from someone else. Be gentle, be kind, be a beautiful soul, and you will make a larger impact than you may ever know. Respect is vital, not just earning it but giving it too. For some, basic aspects of respect may be new and require attention and effort, while they may come more naturally for others. We are all capable of making habit of respectful acts, and we should!

Respect Basics. If you don't already use these respect basics out of habit, fear not. You can train and transition yourself into acting with respect daily, which will allow you to begin building and growing into a respectful and respected person.

Classy Character:

Have character. That means acting selflessly and considering others' thoughts and feelings as well as consequences before acting. Having class means handling situations with grace and a pleasant, level-headed demeanor. Basically, be a person who could be easily liked and trusted because of how you act. Remember, you don't have to necessarily change your personality. I want you to be true to yourself. If you are a goofball or jokester, that's fine! Find ways to appropriately incorporate those into situations. The ability to make others laugh and smile is a valuable one. Just remember to do it with consideration of others and with positivity.

Manners and moral:

Remember to incorporate basic manners, which again means considering others. Acting with moral and manners is something everyone is capable of. Different situations require different types of manners and accept various types of morals. Become a good judge of what is appropriate and when in order to gain simple respect for positive and trustworthy behaviors.

Be trustworthy and patient:

Remember how important it is to keep promises, allow others to feel comfortable in your presence, and maintain patience and a positive attitude. These are things that will make others want to work with you or be around you in various situations. They will respect you for this!

Use Common sense:

Gaining and giving respect are really just a game of common sense. You know how to act and how to treat others, and if you don't, you can easily observe or learn how. Take time and care to just do the right thing. Respect will come on its own if you are a good person.

Be humble and intentional:

If you mess up, admit it. Don't stop at apologizing for wrongdoings, but rather make the necessary changes to right your wrongs and insure others it will not happen again. Embrace differences in opinion, thoughts, and lifestyles. Living with that type of humility and intention will allow you to open your heart and mind in ways you never imagined, as well as allow others to fully trust and respect you. It will feel so great!

The worst thing you can do in your journey of growth is to allow fear to blind others to how magnificent you are. Belittling others, acting with rudeness or cruelty, closing your mind or your heart, are all things that those who are weak use to give the impression of strength. People see through that, though, and you will never reach your dreams or live with true happiness if you mask your greatness.

Giving and gaining respect is an ongoing process. You are allowed to mess up, as long as you make it right. You will encounter people who have not yet mastered these steps to earn and give respect, and you mustn't stress over their behaviors. You are responsible for your own behaviors, and if you are doing it right, others will begin to mimic you and respect will spread like wildfire!

Reflections on respect: *Consult the list above of useful positive intentions and even the reminders of respectful actions. You circled a few to begin focusing on today. Write some thoughts on how you can (in what situations or daily routines) begin implementing those respectful actions:*

Before reading this chapter, what was your outlook on respect (giving and receiving)?

How do you feel you can alter your treatment of others, your actions, your reactions, your intentions to gain more respect from others?

Additional thoughts and comments on respect and its role in your journey:

Part 7

Share Greatness

The Art of Selflessness. Take it from me, when you begin to put others first you will feel a peacefulness that frees you. It feels jubilant and even empowering to share your passions with others, share your knowledge, and encourage others to do the same. Positivity and excitement are highly contagious and motivating! For driven people it can sometimes be difficult to remember to put others first, as determination often puts us in a blinded lane leading directly to our goal, eye on the prize and nothing else. The minute you let others in to be a part of your learning and growing process and focus on building up every aspect of your journey and those involved, you will find joy. Including others and encompassing all aspects of greatness from the respect aspect to the leadership one, from inclusion and positivity to focus and drive can take a focused effort depending on what kind of person you are and how many inner changes you will need to make.

It may seem opposite of what you would expect, but you need to stop pushing, forcing, trying too hard to find greatness and happiness. Sometimes we try so hard we lose ourselves, are blinded, or forget to be good and savor the moments that we become lost and our road map becomes askew. Don't allow that type of ambition to consume you, and begin focusing on building each of the aspects we have discussed so far, and a happiness will come naturally, leading to success, and leading to a contagious and positive greatness.

Think back now to a time when you helped someone or someone

helped you, whether in a big way or something small that has remained embedded in your memory. Think of a feel good moment and reflect on it.

What would an outsider looking in at that moment have observed? What would they have learned, felt, or thought? Use the space below to reflect:

How did that moment make you feel?

Don't fear collaboration. Collaboration is the ability to work with others on a project or task. It is a valuable skill to possess and is useful in numerous settings from a job or career, to participating on an athletic team, to completing a project. As you build your skills, become a leader, and start to share your greatness, try collaborating with other inspirational humans to expand your great ideas!

Another great way to share greatness is to use it to do good things. For example, I use my small business and position as a community leader to bring awareness to local non-profit organizations, as well as domestic and global efforts. You too can generate a ripple effect of positivity using your goals, efforts, and expertise as a catalyst.

For example: If you're good at a sport try volunteering for a little league team to help children learn your sport. An experience like that will teach you just as much as you teach the kids or people you are working with.

Collaboration is a combination of working with others to learn from them, to teach them, and to grow your portfolio of skills. It is a great means to networking and is an opportunity to practice respect, leadership, and other skills you are continuously working to build and improve. Many people unfortunately view volunteering as a chore, something they don't have time for, but if you use it as an additional way to build your craft and gain experience, it will be enjoyable and truly rewarding for all involved. Collaborating with others (whether through volunteering or not) is great because you have the ability to control your time commitment and your capacity of involvement. So, even if on a small scale, start collaborating!

What is something (a skill, a passion, knowledge) you have right now that you could share with someone else or use to help someone else?

How will sharing that skill (or passion, or knowledge) benefit you? How would it benefit others?

Part 8

Find the Super G in you!

Before you Create a Master Plan. You know by now that you are never too young or too old to start your journey to happiness and success. We all create life plans, road maps, and change them throughout life. Those plans change often. We add extra steps and sometimes even change our destinations and change them again. All of that is normal and even expected, and your goal from this moment on is to use everything you see, hear, every flat tire moment, every monumental moment, every experience as a tool to learn, grow, and change. Continuously grow and change, and use intention to build your skills. You have reviewed many valuable tools to help you along your path, many of which you probably already held knowledge of but needed a reminder on. The concrete changes and actions are somewhat simpler to accomplish than some of the inner changes; those can be tough. Be sure to be honest with yourself, though, and really work to the core to cleanse your soul in order to travel forth with a clear and positive mind. Review the following purifying behaviors, and apply whichever are necessary requisites for your purposes. Just be honest with yourself.

Find the strength to let go. One of the most difficult steps toward growing yourself is the one where you have to let go of things that are holding you back. Sometimes cutting ties with the past, letting go of anger, or distancing ourselves from someone (or even multiple people) who we care for but are holding us back are the most difficult by far. You will need to be completely honest with yourself right now in beginning the process of determining what things are helping propel you in a positive direction through life and which are keeping you from moving forward or are drowning your efforts in negativity. It is a delicate understanding of your personal priorities and what or who is most important to you. It is all your decision. Take a long, thorough look at the list of potential positive influences in your life. I want you to mark and make notes, comments, and reflections where useful to you. Really try and discover what influences currently active in your life are bettering your journey and adding positive light to your goals and efforts. People, hobbies, even physical things that bring you joy or put a smile on your face are great to keep around, but those that cause unnecessary stress, sadness, or create barriers between you and your goals should be eliminated or altered in a way to create passage to happiness. I encourage you to be truthful to yourself during this evaluation. Don't let jealousy of others or deflection of anger cause you to cut ties with someone who may actually be beneficial to have in your life.

Think now of those positive influences. Note specific people, hobbies, existing things in your life that are truly assets in your journey.

Positive Influences: Keep these around!

- People who fully support your ideas and goals. These people offer useful advice, and helpful opinions but do not doubt you and your plans:

- A job/career you thoroughly enjoy (note what you enjoy about it). Even if there is space to grow within the job or you don't plan on being there forever, it somehow is providing you comfort or positivity within your realm of growth goals:

- People who are providing support in the way of donating funding to your goals, providing their time and/or services to help your progress, providing guidance of some sort to help you progress:

- Groups, clubs, regular social meetings, or volunteer groups you are involved with. Though these take your time, they are often a safe haven to share your thoughts and get feedback, and they often provide a sort of escape from reality to something you enjoy:

- Physical things that are helping your journey. I don't often encourage dependence or seeking comfort in physical things, but something like a stable home, reliable car, a reading nook or work station, etc. may provide just the right positive vibes and space for you to maintain peace and positivity:

- A hobby that adds positive experience, stress relief, or just sheer joy to your life:

- Any other person, experience, or opportunity you feel grateful to have that is allowing you to continue in a forward and positive motion toward building your life:

Now, I will ask you to complete the same steps considering things that could be holding you back, and it is sometimes difficult to be completely honest when doing this for fear of losing something or someone who has been a part of your life for an extended amount of time. Just be honest. This thought process is strictly for you and no one else. Eliminating negatives will lift weight from your shoulders and make you stronger. Read through possible negativities and mark, comment, and reflect on those you feel exist in your current world and efforts to build and grow.

<u>Negative influences: Cut these loose</u>, distance yourself, or express (to people) the importance of a change from negative to positive in them.

- People who don't believe in your dreams, intentions, and goals. Are they jealous? Are they unwilling to assist or believe it will be too much work? Do they lack the drive you have?

- An addiction or bad habit. This could be a substance addiction or a recurring habit you have that is negative or not aiding your progression in any way (or that someone close to you has that is influencing your success):

- A person (or people) who intentionally makes efforts to tear you down, create drama or negativity, or hurt you in order to hold you back and keep you from growing and becoming successful (Is it a boss? A spouse or significant other? Is it a jealous friend or person? Who is it?):

- Concerns, fears, doubts, and what-ifs. It is normal to have these, but you can't let them completely stop you. Instead, you have to begin thinking of how to overcome them or work around them:

- A stereotype or belief that creates obstacles or brings negativity. This could be a disease or disability, gender stereotypes, race stereotypes, etc.:

- Anything else you can think of that you can cut from your life or encourage to change in order for you to move forward positively and successfully:

Before you move on in this program, I want you to go back to your list of positive influences and skim through it again. Recognize that, even if you were only able to think of one single positive influence, the positives are so powerful. Those people are there for you. Those jobs, possessions, groups, hobbies, whatever it was are on your team! Be so grateful and draw motivation, inspiration, and positivity from those things to help you overcome the negatives. I truly believe that every single positive, no matter how small, has the potential to outweigh multiple negatives. Use that to your benefit!

Overcome: You can do it! Are you working through an experience that halted your life happiness or has kept you from reaching your goals in life? You already know that my Multiple Sclerosis diagnosis had great potential to keep me from reaching my goals, but I am now asking you to do what I did and use those experiences to emerge an even stronger, wiser person that much closer to your goals. You can't let those negativities hold you back. You may be thinking to yourself, "How can I do that, Gina? How can I ever get past this moment, this negative thing?" I understand. I had those moments and same thoughts, for sure, where I wondered how I could ever go on, move forward, get past it. My MS diagnosis wasn't the only time. Going through a divorce, losing friends or family, struggling financially, building a small business from the ground up (a terrifying feat), and so many other large and small moments where I really believed I should give up have acted as mere speed bumps in my life.

If you take nothing else from this program, take this: You can do it, and you will. I believe in you, and I know that anything is possible. Believe those words with me. Repeat to yourself, "I can, and I will!" It is never the end. One set back may lead to a changed path on your road map, but the journey does not end there. One path may become blocked, then another, and another until you start to believe you are out of routes, but I am here to tell you that if you run out of planned routes create a dirt road if you have to! If it is something you want badly enough you will find a way to get from point A to point B. You may have to work harder or it may take longer than intended, but you can get there and you will. Just believe. Use all you have started to build through this program, your clear goal, your newfound leadership skills, your ability to use experiences for positive, to build momentum and get inspired. When you start believing, living with intention and drive, exuding positivity, and living as a good human being, it will all start happening for you. It really will.

Stop blaming and take ownership. Something that takes true courage and strength is the act of admitting your own wrongs, getting to the root of the problem, and deflecting blame unnecessarily onto others. As a child, did you ever experience another kid blaming you for something you didn't do? I did, and I remember how I felt so betrayed by the other child and how surprised I felt at the unfair act. It was cruel and terrible through the eyes of a child, even though it was most likely something frivolous like who left a toy laying on the floor in the playroom. It didn't feel good to be wrongfully accused as a child, and it is even worse as an adult. Sometimes we place blame on others to avoid the grueling truth that we are at fault. I've recognized more and more on my journey that many adults find it difficult to diagnose the root of unhappiness, anger, sadness, or problems we experience, so ricocheting blame onto someone else creates a temporary escape from those feelings or issues. In doing that, the person receiving the wrongful blame is caused feelings of betrayal, unfairness, hurt, and all those feelings he felt as a child when he was wrongfully blamed. Constantly blaming others for your own unhappiness will only make matters worse. You will begin causing arguments, losing loved ones, causing others to feel uneasy or uncomfortable in your presence, and worst of all you will only grow more and more unhappy. Instead, you must take a serious look at what the root of your unease is in order to begin repairing the problem. Stop blaming others. Sometimes they are fuel to your fire, so to speak, but continuously playing the victim while pointing fingers is not healthy. There is nothing wrong with admitting you need help, or a change, or that you messed up. You can make it right and you can make changes. You will feel better once you recognize the true issues and work toward mending them.

Anger, Temper, and Others. In addition to accepting responsibility for your own actions and feelings rather than blaming others, you must avoid taking your anger out on others. It happens to everyone.

Humans can endure a lot, but sometimes we snap under too much stress or pressure. Unfortunately, it is easy to turn our implosions into explosions that hurt or affect those around us. It is not healthy to hold stress and anger in, but it is equally unhealthy to lose your cool on an innocent bystander.

Not too long ago I was working an event for the non-profit I was working part time for. I had spent months planning the event and hours working the event that day. Despite the uncomfortable MS symptoms I sometimes feel after consecutive hours of physical activity, I worked through the entire event without a single complaint. I handled very rude volunteers, unorganized leaders, large crowds (which can be stressful for MSers), and just an overall exhausting event with a smile on my face and extreme enthusiasm. I was grateful for the event, happy to see so many people there to support, and happy to help. At the end of the day, one of my fellow co-workers, who was clearly very stressed out and exhausted, finally snapped and lost her temper. Unfortunately for me, I was the only person near enough to her for her to yell at. She said truly heartbreakingly cruel things to me, rather she screamed them at me. I should tell you, I had been working for them for months as a sort of favor, knowing they needed help from someone with my experience, and I cared deeply for the organization. I walked away from my co-worker that day, instantly ready to forgive her knowing she was displacing anger. A simple apology would have cured the entire situation. In this case, she chose to place blame elsewhere and never apologized, but you don't have to make that same mistake. We all snap. A simple apology can go a long way in a situation like that. The real problem occurs when someone continuously takes ongoing anger or unhappiness out on others. This goes along with displacing blame.

Instead of allowing yourself to lose your temper on someone else, try doing the following when you are overwhelmed, stressed out, or angry about something:

- Take a few deep breaths, step back from whatever it is that is causing your unease, and clear your mind.
- Pep-talk yourself by reminding yourself that whatever it is that is happening in that moment only feels overwhelming but will be okay in the end. You can get through it. Just calm down.
- Make a joke. This sounds silly, I know, but I rely on my sense of humor to pull me through numerous tough times, and it works extra well in those "close to breaking" moments. If you can find anything at all humorous, ironic, or silly about the situation pinpoint it!
- Rather than lashing out on those surrounding you, allow them to help you through that moment. The people surrounding us are often participating in the same experience we are and can help in some way to make it a little easier. We can all help each other.
- Lower your voice and adjust your attitude. Sometimes when we lose control, we yell at someone else (or even just yell in general) which can infuriate us further. Our own anger can feed on itself! Then others attempting to calm us just add fuel, and it is a downward spiral from there. Before you snap or even right after your initial outburst, try lowering your voice or changing your tone. That in itself has the ability to calm you down.
- Remaining calm and level-headed when others are yelling, angry, or chaotic has the power to cool an entire situation. Give it a try!

Are you someone who loses your temper easily or do you tend to hold in your anger? Reflect on how you handle anger from being overwhelmed or stressed out. Is it working for you or do you need to make changes? Reflect here:

It is very important to never take your anger out on someone unnecessarily. Learn to manage your stress to eliminate explosive moments like those.

Managing Stress. I will admit that I have experienced more "this is my breaking point" moments this past year than ever before. It is seriously like one thing after another has gone wrong, large and small. Financial struggles, added work hours and responsibilities, all the typical stressful things have been piled on my life-plate this year, causing me to feel its weight. It has taken immense concentration and practice to perfect my ability to laugh off struggles, allow others to keep me calm and hold my hand through overwhelming moments, and never take my anger out on others. I will be the first to tell you it feels so satisfying to be able to remain positive, smiling, kind, and cheerful even in the midst of turmoil.

I have learned so many new ways to handle and manage stress, and I want to share them with you. Try using them and observing your own methods as you continue on your journey. Try to be conscious and make intentional efforts to improve at handling stressful situations. Add those moments to your list of useful experiences to empower and strengthen you.

- Try to stay organized by using calendars and schedules to plan. Make good use of your time by planning and staying on task using those organizational tools.
- Tidy and organize your home, workspace, or office. Believe it or not, a clean and organized space generates a more clean and organized soul and eliminates unnecessary stress or tension.
- Instead of feeling sorry for yourself, make the situation better. Take ownership by making a plan, doing whatever you can to better the situation, and use your resources. A resolution may not happen immediately, but feeling a bit in control is much better than feeling completely defeated. Pouting and feeling sorry for yourself creates no forward progress for yourself.
- Eliminate Self-induced stresses! I can't express enough how important this is. An example of this would be having an

argument with your boss at work then bringing that anger home, holding on to it, and allowing it to consume your thoughts and mood for an extended amount of time. It isn't healthy or helpful. Instead, brush it off however you can, talk about it, write about it, or generate a plan to rectify the situation with your boss. Let it go. Another example would be allowing yourself to feel overwhelmingly stressed out over tiny, unimportant things. For example, someone spills a drink on your carpet, and you completely lose your temper, allow it to affect your mood, and allow your mood to affect those around you. That is all unnecessary. Look at the bigger picture in situations to determine whether your cause of stress is self-induced. A spill on the carpet is not the end of your world and is certainly not the most unfortunate thing you could possibly experience in life. You may certainly feel frustrated with it or a sense of urgency in cleaning it. It may even require disciplinary action for whoever spilled it, but it is something you have a choice to brush off. Eliminate self-induced stress!

- If others are offering to help, let them! Even if someone else completes a task and gets to the same end result in a different manner than you, let them help. Each person has a routine way to clean dishes, for example, but in the end the dishes are cleaned no matter what. So, if you are overwhelmed and stressed out and someone offers to do the dishes for you to help alleviate some of your to-do list, let them! Let go of your need to have everything done a specific way. The dishes will be cleaned, and that will be one less thing you had to do. Let people help you!

- One thing at a time. Handle responsibilities one task at a time, and handle unexpected circumstances the same! Sometimes looking at my to-do list causes instant anxiety and a sense of defeat. No way I can finish all of that! Try focusing on one item at a time. It is much easier to manage one task at a time than forty-five of them.

- If it is something beyond your control, do not let it ruin you! It can make you upset, or angry, and you may even have a mild breakdown over it, but get yourself together and start figuring out how to work that new moment into your plan. Flexibility is important in handling stresses.

- Remember you can handle more than you think you can. Your limits may be pushed and pushed, but you are resilient and capable! Take some breaths and push forward!

What other ways of handling and managing stress have you used? Which are you willing to try or think will work for you? Reflect here:

Stop feeling sorry. I said it already, but it is one of those things we sometimes don't even realize we are doing. Don't allow yourself to feel sorry for yourself. You may have it tough. You may be experiencing more difficulty than you ever imagined possible. It is completely acceptable to recognize that fact, but you cannot continuously feel sorry for yourself. Pouting, seeking sympathy from others, using your circumstance as an excuse to victimize yourself, none of those are useful or respectable. Remember, people are constantly fighting battles that you may not even know about, and you are not the only one experiencing struggles in life. It is okay to seek help or to feel sad, but you can't expect others to handle your struggles for you. Like a toddler, throwing a tantrum is not useful in any way and often makes the toddler and those around her unhappy and uncomfortable. Don't be an adult throwing a tantrum. Get it together and show those struggles who's boss!

Listen to others. This can be so challenging. Our closest friends and loved ones often hesitate to tell us when they observe struggles needing attention in us. They don't want to upset or anger us, or cause us to feel rallied against. It can feel embarrassing to have someone we care about express their concern for us. It can also cause you to feel bullied or betrayed when they voice worries. If someone you care about comes to you with concern of your behaviors, moods, actions or reactions, listen to them. Others who know you well are often able to realize changes in you before you even do or before you are able to admit them to yourself. Don't get angry with someone for expressing concern, as they are only trying to help you. They typically do not feel superior to you in any way but truly care and want happiness and success for you. Denying a change in moods or behaviors will only create repetitive moods and behaviors. If you are expressing negative behaviors or moods due to personal stresses or unhappiness, those will only continue until changed. You have to recognize them before you are able to work on changing or bettering them, so if someone who cares for you notices a negative behavior or mood, listen to them and work toward fixing the issue. This goes back to getting to the root of the problem in order to truly and more permanently repair it.

Pep-talk yourself. I am proud to say that I am getting rather skilled at positive pep-talking myself through tough times. Something as miniscule as breaking a finger nail, losing an earring, or finding the television remote batteries dead can be enough to push us past our limits when life is already piling upon our shoulders. In addition to practicing managing stress and staying calm, simply learning the art of self-pep-talking is valuable. Seriously. Sometimes a simple, "you got this!" can go a long way. Sometimes hearing ourselves reminding ourselves that we can make it past any given moment is more motivational than anyone else telling us we can. Don't be afraid to encourage yourself. Work on being positive in those moments, rather than negative. There is already enough negative around you and in the world, you don't need to exude negativity upon yourself as well. Pep-talks work in locker rooms before important competitions, and they work in your own mind in challenging moments.

Reaching your goals and finding true happiness is so much more attainable with a clear and positive mind, heart, and soul. Doing these little things will act in your favor along your path. Try to focus and make conscious efforts to improve how you handle and react to stress, how you treat and listen to others, and what type of mood and attitude you portray and exude, and your trip along your roadmap will only get better and better. You will have an opportunity to plan your roadmap with as little or as much guidance as you prefer in the next section of this book. It is important to continuously record and recognize your strengths, your weaknesses, your goals, your thoughts, and your ideas. All of those things will continuously change, so you must continuously observe them and change with them as needed. Use your observations to guide your path, draw inspiration from them and from others, and share yourself with the world.

I shared with you before a story of how I gained the nickname "Super G" and what that name means to me. My self-reinvention began in my early thirties because of the traumatizing life-event of being diagnosed with Multiple Sclerosis, you already knew that. You don't have to experience something traumatizing to boost your reinvention. You can start now. I think everyone deserves an opportunity to harness their inner Super G and at the moment that is right for each! So here you are. Get excited, continuously revisit the useful tips and tools you have begun to explore in the parts of this program, and let's build your future!

Self-reinvention. What does that mean? Self-reinvention is something that most people actually do multiple times throughout life, even if they don't realize they are doing it. It is an opportunity to alter yourself, to adapt to new surroundings or experiences, to travel your road map. You aren't changing every single thing about you, instead you are keeping those fantastic qualities that are bettering you as a person and adding to them. Adapting to your surroundings, while maintaining who you are is perfectly natural.

In middle and high school we are surrounded by a group of peers, teachers, and family with opportunities to grow and find ourselves within the confinements of that particular group of people. It is a necessary time in life to experience hardships, innocence, learn skills and gain knowledge, and it is a time to really invent who we want to be known as. Leaving high school, whether you attend college or not, is a time to take with you the persona you created for yourself in high school and grow and build upon it. In college, in the military, in a job or career your high school self moves along that road map experiencing new things and transforming along the way, keeping their persona intact but adding to it and altering it in ways. That adaptation is usually a person's first big reinvention. Post-high school experiences tend to change us greatly. Likewise, graduating college, getting married, or having children are typically the next big reinventions. With each phase in life you keep parts of your previous persona and add new elements to adapt you to life's newest challenges and experiences. It is all a natural part of life.

The moment you realize you haven't accomplished everything you had hoped, experience tragedy, or feel you are not truly happy is the moment you can make a choice to reinvent yourself. All of the skills and advice given in this program can be used in the natural progression of life and in your own decision to reinvent yourself. I still remain almost completely the person I was prior to my MS diagnosis, but I have chosen to reinvent myself into a better person with more abilities to generate change, create happiness, make an impact, and gain personal happiness. It is up to you how much of your previous self you want to take with you into this new phase of life and how much you want to change or better yourself. Use your reflections and the important elements provided in this book to help you decide which parts of you will benefit your new persona and which will hold you back. Shed those that will weigh you down and build upon the ones that will only add to your happiness and success.

I had to shed a lot of my doubt and uncertainty. I had to learn forgiveness and understanding. The most difficult step for me was the learning to shed my anger. I took with me an existing passion for helping others and experiences with doing just that. It is completely up to you what stays and what goes. Sometimes it is difficult to let go of parts of yourself, but you should understand that it is necessary in order to free yourself enough to grow into the person you want to be. It takes courage and strength, which you have.

Using your reflections from previous parts of this program, reflect on personal assets you feel will benefit you in the reinvention of yourself and which you feel would weigh you down, hold you back, or generate unnecessary negativity.

List personal traits you feel will benefit you as you reinvent yourself and build your new life road map:

List personal traits or experiences you feel you need to let go of or alter completely in order to positively move forward:

Step Two

Get started!

Part 9

Get Organized and Prepare your Foundation

Get organized. Even if you aren't typically an organization genius, you must first get organized before proceeding toward your goals. Organizing your tasks and your personal life will help eliminate unnecessary stress. Organize in ways that fit your lifestyle and personality. I use journals and a physical planner book to organize because I am the type of person who likes being able to write and doodle my lists and appointments. You may choose to keep detailed electronic calendars and lists. Do whatever works for you so that you are more likely to stick with it and create a routine with it. If you are already a very organized person, great! Stick with it! If this is new territory for you, don't worry! You will learn to love it. Here are some helpful hints to get you organized:

- Get a calendar or planner of your choice, whether hard copy or electronic
- Begin by writing down or scheduling something simple like when to pay regular bills or complete routine tasks

  - For example: I attend the same workout every single Monday morning at 5:30a.m., so I may start my organizing by writing in my calendar "Workout at 5:35a.m." on each Monday for the entire month.

- Think of tasks you can begin working toward now. For example, if you hope to begin completing volunteer experiences at a local non-profit designate specific times and days on your schedule to complete those tasks. It is more likely that you will successfully complete these items if you intentionally choose times to do so. When I am writing a book I always add in my calendar days and time frames designated to writing. It makes it feel more like a commitment that must be completed.

- Create checklists that you can physically mark off as completed. I've known people who choose to hang a whiteboard or chalkboard somewhere in their houses where they can write a day's tasks and check them off as completed. I write a list at the start of each work day at my boutique and leave it on my front counter so that I can mark items off as they are completed. It becomes a sort of goal in itself to complete the entire list in the day. It gives a sense of accomplishment and positive movement in the right direction.

- Create a long term list somewhere easily accessible. I keep a small page in the front of my calendar book with larger goals that will take longer so that I see them at the start of each day. For example: Written on my long-term goal list is "Publish Book #2." That is not a task I could complete in one day, so I list it on my long term list to remember what I am ultimately working toward. I also have long-term sales goals and charitable donation goals for my store written on that list. It motivates me to complete the small everyday tasks necessary to reach those larger goals.

What other ways of organizing can you think of that may benefit you on your journey? Write some ideas down or come back to it when you think of something!

Prepare your Foundation. I would suggest polishing your foundation before building on it. What I mean is that it wouldn't hurt to make sure your personal life is free of clutter before adding to it. Here are some suggestions. Write your thoughts and ideas to help you remember which you find useful:

- Spruce up your health and wellness: I'm not talking about a diet or losing weight. I truly believe that eating healthy and being as active as we can leads to a happier us! I love relieving stress with a good workout or outdoor activity, and I always feel so energetic and in a better mood when I eat clean and healthy foods regularly. Try it, you may like it!

- Give your house a deep clean or organize a room: Removing clutter and cleaning house is no fun for most of us, but if you're like me you feel so much better sitting down to relax in a clean and organized room!

- Create a workspace: This may not apply to you and your personal goals, but many goals and tasks require working on a computer, writing something down, reading or researching, or other activities that require a space to do that. Create a clean and organized space designated as your work space. Make it somewhere you get excited to be and can really let your ideas soar! I enjoy doing a large amount of work at a local coffee shop!

- Get a journal: Even if it is just a small notepad, try keeping a type of journal or notebook with you to jot down ideas or important information on the go. I have a designated journal for my writing project that I carry with me. It makes it easy to pull the journal out of my bag and quickly write down new thoughts or potentially great ideas that I may want to incorporate in my books! Plus, it's fun to pick out new journals or even personalize one!

- Prepare any inspiration boards, calendars, and other organization tools you have chosen to use: Have your tools all ready to go before you really start gaining momentum so that it is all readily available for your use.

- Make amends and tie up loose ties: If there is anything weighing on your mind that can be mended, do it! Forgiving someone, apologizing, or having a difficult discussion to resolve a serious issue or disagreement is rarely a fun task, but your mind will function more freely and your thoughts will flow more clearly without the constant stress of unresolved issues constantly hovering.
- Begin intentionally doing good deeds: You may already do this type of thing, but if not you should start now! Can you pay it forward by purchasing coffee for the customer behind you at the coffee shop? Can you compliment someone (and mean it)? Can you make a contribution or congratulate someone? Any little thing you can do to add positivity and good vibes to your life, do them!

Now you are ready to begin crafting a plan! Remember, your road map is flexible and can be changed as needed. I often come up with new ideas that stem from others and have learned the importance of flexibility in order to improve tasks along the way. Not to mention, as humans our interests, goals, and desires often change as we grow and experience life, so our road maps must adapt as well.

The process of forming your road map will consist of knowing and creating a clear statement of an ultimate goal (or more than one) and then breaking that down into smaller goals to avoid feeling overwhelmed or overlooking vital steps in the process. Each person's goals are different, so you will always need to adjust this program to fit your personal needs. Before you write your goals down allow me to provide an example. I will use the time I decided to build and open a small business.

Ultimate Goal: Open a specialized clothing and gift boutique.
*I may even choose to list a goal for an opening
date or desired location for the business.*

Next, I would list steps I must take to meet that ultimate goal. You may find as you go that you need to change the order of operation of your steps to take or add or remove some steps. This should always be a working list, growing and changing.

Checklist of steps to take:

Research

- **Permits needed**
- **Average business loan amount needed**
- **Potential brands to carry in the store**
- **Possible locations**
- **Website and social media needs**
- **Business Name**
- **Business logo**

Your steps to take checklist may be very long or it may be short, and you can list as much detail as you want. Each of the items in my example involve lengthy descriptions and details, so I kept it simple.

If you are working on multiple life changes at once, be sure to keep your visions and tasks organized accordingly. It is acceptable, however, to work toward multiple goals at once. When I was diagnosed with MS I began working toward goals of opening my own business and was also working toward improving my mental and physical health all while writing a book. Being truly happy and successful rarely involves making only one change. It is totally up to you how many tasks and goals you want to handle at once.

You will also be able to use the coming pages as an organizational tool. We will identify a clear goal and list of supporting steps for you to take to reach that goal (or multiple goals). We will also pull information from previous steps to tie in with your goals, creating an ultimate growing guide. We will end with the creation of a master road map for you to follow! Let's get started!

First, identify a clear ultimate goal to use as your guiding light!

Find your

Write your

ULTIMATE GOAL.

below:

SUPER G

Now, write supporting steps to reach your ultimate goal: (Remember, it is up to you how much or little detail you put in this list).

Next, you will need to break down each of the steps you need to take. For example, my first step toward opening my own business was to do research. So, after creating my list of steps I would then need to break down each step to plan what will need to be done with each step. You can choose how much detail to go into here. You will always add and change ideas as you go, so don't feel obligated to try and master every detail of every single item on your list! Maybe your list looks more like a life plan, like this:

Ultimate Goal: Have a career that I truly enjoy and a stable income.
Steps to take:
-Go to college, training, get certified, or apply for the job
-Become more skilled at XYZ in order to earn a promotion or move into a new position
-Save X amount of money each month to later use for a new, more reliable car

Regardless of what your road map is leading you to, you need to recognize each of the steps required to move smoothly along the path. Taking your time and breaking tasks down into smaller progressive steps eliminates feeling overwhelmed, plus it gives us more opportunities to celebrate small victories when tasks are accomplished. Use the pages provided to map out your steps or create your own template. Your plan should be crafted your way! Use the next pages to begin diving into small tasks you can begin to complete, whether it's something like applying to colleges, starting a fundraiser to fund your ultimate goal, sit down and write, whatever it is! Use your steps toward reaching your ultimate goal as a guide. These note pages are for you to begin exploring. You should look at your ultimate goal and steps list to begin jotting down the tasks you know you need to work toward. Then, you may choose to transfer your thoughts to a personal journal, electronic list, or other personalized place to keep your thoughts organized.

Always work with your ultimate goal in mind! Start exploring!

Remember, these notes are for you and no one else. Alter them when you want and how you want!

Step ___ Breakdown

Use this space to write notes and plan how to conquer your first step toward happiness!
Hint: Use lists, and take as many pages as you need!

You're doing great! Keep the thoughts flowing!

I can.
I will.

Step ___ Breakdown

Use this space to write notes and plan how to conquer your first step toward happiness!
Hint: Use lists, and take as many pages as you need!

Keep it up! Remember, you can and will accomplish these tasks!
Have you looked at your ultimate goal lately? Keep your eyes on the prize!

Step ___ Breakdown

Use this space to write notes and plan how to conquer your first step toward happiness!
Hint: Use lists, and take as many pages as you need!

Step ___ Breakdown

Use this space to write notes and plan how to conquer your first step toward happiness!
Hint: Use lists, and take as many pages as you need!

Step ___ Breakdown

Use this space to write notes and plan how to conquer your first step toward happiness!
Hint: Use lists, and take as many pages as you need!

Step ___ Breakdown

Use this space to write notes and plan how to conquer your first step toward happiness!
Hint: Use lists, and take as many pages as you need!

I can.
I will.

Step ___ Breakdown

Use this space to write notes and plan how to conquer your first step toward happiness!
Hint: Use lists, and take as many pages as you need!

Now, you don't want to become so engrossed in writing notes and thoughts that you forget all the other important steps to gaining happiness and success. Remember all those other important steps? Try incorporating the necessary steps toward things like becoming a better leader or becoming a more selfless, caring person into your lists and notes. Next, we will spend some time focusing on those other tasks in efforts to transition them into a daily routine that will only assist your efforts to tackling your goals! In the end we will combine all your efforts and thoughts to create a master, working map!

Part 10

Incorporate Necessary Tools

Potential

Remember all those other tools, skills, and traits you took the time to study in previous chapters? We need to cycle those back into the mix here. You answered questions, wrote reflections, and began to understand yourself with each of the tools I told you were important toward obtaining happiness. You will now briefly revisit those in order to incorporate them into your road map. Remember, those skills were things you can start to improve and incorporate slowly and as you go. It isn't necessary to stress yourself out over a hard and quick change. Take your time and incorporate that personal growth into your daily life. It helps to plan and add them to your goals lists and road map so they are not forgotten.

We will first hop all the way back to Part 2 where we started to discover your potentials and what exactly that means. That chapter included not only advice on finding your own true potential but opening your eyes to potentials around. Potential leadership opportunities, potential support team members, potential life changes, and more! Those things you have potential to be great at are probably linked to your goals, as well. Most of our passions and interests go hand in hand with our potentials, which is why we are interested in them! You need to pinpoint those specific potentials and start to build and shape them into accomplishments that fit in with your life plans.

They're right there all the time, those things (or that one thing) that you feel within you that you know you are great at or could be great at, but the world just may not see it yet. <u>List some of the potential you have that can directly benefit your plans and goals when harnessed correctly:</u>

Remember that ultimate goal and list of supporting steps to reach that goal? Revisit that now, and keep revisiting it as frequently as possible. Now, I want you to write a statement, an assertive and confident statement of one of your potential skills, actions, or greatness that directly fit into your plan. Here's an example:

I have the potential to raise $15,000 this year for various charities by organizing fundraisers, selling items, and generating awareness. How this fits into my plan: I want to own a successful business that is known for charitable involvement and truly makes a difference. I have a goal to give back 1 million dollars through my business, and my potential to raise $15,000 this year is a step toward that goal.

In that example, I started with a simple and short statement of my solid potential. I then explained briefly how that potential fits into my overall plan. Though raising $15,000 is far less than the overall goal, it shows forward progress and provides opportunities for me to continuously harness my potential to organize fundraisers and raise funding various ways. As I learn and grow I can expect my statement to change each year until I eventually reach my ultimate goal of raising 1 million dollars for charities. Now you try:

Statement of Potential:

How this fits into the ultimate plan:

In Part 2 we discussed potential to unlocking success. You understand now how to determine what potential you have that directly ties to your ultimate plans. What other potential is out there for you? I want you to take a moment to think back (or even revisit your responses) to Part 2 and pinpoint the potential that exists within you to find success, greatness, and happiness. Write them down below and start to connect that potential with your ultimate plan and steps you are taking to improve your life and reach your goals!

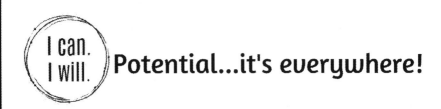

I can. I will. Potential...it's everywhere!

What is your potential?
It may be skills, opportunities, actions, feelings or growth as a
person, or impacts.
Write your thoughts here:

How will harnessing your potential get your closer to reaching
your goals?

Part 11

Incorporate Necessary Tools

Experiences

I can almost guarantee that good and bad experiences of various shapes and sizes have visited you even in the time since you read Part 3 of this book. Part 3 was full of advice on why it is important to use every single experience as a growing opportunity and how to do that. When reading that chapter you most likely thought to yourself about the great things and the terrible that you have lived through. You may have even thought of family or people close to you who have experienced great tragedy or those who have had great success. Allowing your mind to recall those things or expand thoughts on moments is a very useful tool, but now you will put it on paper to better recognize your own growth from experiences and how it will directly relate to your life progression. You may need more space than what is provided to really dig into all the valuable lessons you have learned from life experiences, and that is just fine! Use what you need, and remember you should always revisit, add to, and pull from each and every process, idea, and moment as you go. It is an ongoing process. Emerging into the new you, developing yourself and reaching those goals will take time.

Let's begin with reflecting on some positive moments. Try focusing on just one or two to start. Think of a positive experience (or multiple positives) that you learned from, took value from, and can apply to your self-improvement and journey through life. Now, use the next interactive section to briefly describe those experiences, jot down some of the value you gained from them, and decide how you will use them in your steps toward success.

Experiences:

The Ultimate Growth Tools

Positive Experiences:

Briefly describe one positive experience that added value & joy to your life:

What lesson(s) did you learn, tools did you take, or specific value was gained from the experience you listed?

How will the value, tools, and lessons you listed directly aid your accomplishing your steps toward happiness and success? In other words, how was that experience specifically valuable in your efforts to reach your ultimate goal?

Now you will complete the same steps using a negative experience that impacted your life, left you stronger and with more tools, and will be used positively in your process to reaching success. It is sometimes harder to pull positives from negative events, especially those that occurred recently, but they are there! Think of your negative experience as a plant. I have a beautiful Lilly plant in my boutique that was a gift from my store's opening. I adore nature and truly love having plants in my home and at the store, but I have the most difficult time keeping them alive. Sometimes after coming in from being away from the store for a few days the Lilly plant is drooping and looks almost certainly dead. I always frantically water it, and it never fails that plant perks slowly back to its glorious, full and green self. A negative experience certainly has the potential to break you down to what may feel like your weakest and most vulnerable time. It's those moments that allow defeat and sadness to creep in. Like a plant, drooping and in need of help, if you water your soul with positives you will slowly emerge back to your normal glorious self or sometimes an even more radiant version of yourself.

Finding positives can be so difficult in those toughest times, but try using the following tips to help you. These have worked for me in painful situations small and large!

- While you may have little or no control over some situations you have complete control of how you choose to emerge from them. It is much more difficult to emerge with positivity, but you can do it. It is your choice. You are in control of that, and no one else can take that from you.
- If you are angry about an unfortunate circumstance remember that anger is poisonous. Ingesting poison will only worsen by holding it all in. Let go of the anger, and cleanse your soul in order to move forward.
- You are strong, and you can handle anything. Sometimes it doesn't feel that way, but think of action movies or shows where characters do seemingly impossible things in the midst of disaster. Humans are resilient, and we grow stronger in

devastating times. We do things we never would have thought possible just to survive or save others.

- Learn to delete negatives. Think of a video saved to your computer. You can rewind, and re-watch, and repeat, but it is the same exact video each time. Is it heartbreaking? Is it holding you back or beating you down? Why watch it on repeat? Delete it. Do the same with negatives from experiences.

- Be kind. You are suffering, and that is understandable, but regardless of your own feelings you have to be kind, especially to those who are trying to help or are not in any way involved in what is bringing you down. Taking your anger, frustration, or sadness out on others will only make you feel worse and burn positive bridges. Showing kindness and selflessness in your lowest times is an ultimate sign of strength.

- Put on some good music, something that vibrates your soul and lifts your spirits, pull yourself together, and leave that terrible moment behind you.

- Try not to focus on only the bad things. Yes, sometimes you are forced to reflect or swim in the negatives for a while, but you can find so many positives during that time. For example, if you are in an ongoing custody battle with an ex. It is tearing you down, stressing you out, and worrying you so much it hurts your heart. Look around. There are so many positives surrounding you every single day even in the midst of your anguish. Reach for the positives, cherish them, use them to guide you and pull you through.

- Remember you are never expected to be perfect. The most respected people are those who don't hide their flaws but exemplify how they are working to better them constantly. Just be the best version of yourself you can possibly be, and the world will see you working to rise.

- Take care of yourself. Get rest, mind your health, do small things daily to make yourself happy and calm, and let others be a part of that.

- Never feel inferior. A person holding a Doctorate degree and one who didn't graduate highschool both have equal capabilities of making a positive impact on the world. It all comes down to what kind of person you are, not how much money you made, how many fans you had, or how big your house was. Be good. Do good.
- Be grateful. You are alive, and while you may be struggling, you have things others may not. Yes, others have things you want or need and don't possess, but focus on the gratitude you have for what you do have. Build upon those things.
- You can and will make it. You will look back on tough times one day and be thankful for the experiences. You are stronger and more beautiful than ever because of them.

Experiences:
The Ultimate Growth Tools

Negative Experiences:

Briefly describe one negative experience::

What lesson(s) did you learn, tools did you take, or specific value was gained from the experience you listed?

How will the value, tools, and lessons you listed directly aid your accomplishing your steps toward happiness and success? In other words, how was that experience specifically valuable in your efforts to reach your ultimate goal?

In my opinion, taking value from life experiences is one of the most valuable skills any person continuously growing into a better person can possess. Use the process of pinpointing value taken from experiences to assist your efforts of reaching your goals consistently and continuously. I would suggest intentionally realizing value from experiences whenever possible and noting them or consciously adding them to your personal assets bank to be used throughout your journey. Keep your mind in motion by attentively and intentionally learning useful things to help you accomplish your goals. You are the only person who knows exactly what your dreams are and what would make you truly happy, so it is up to you to collect the knowledge, the skills, anything you can along the path that will help you make those dreams a reality. Using experiences is one of the best ways, it's essentially free and abundant all the time!

Part 12

Incorporate Necessary Tools

Leadership

Have you been working toward improving your leadership skills since we last explored them in Parts 4 and 5? Take whatever steps you can, large or small, to always improve your leadership, which includes your communication skills, decision making, situation management, and more. By acknowledging where leadership will prove specifically valuable throughout the process of reaching your goals, you will better understand exactly what you need to do to improve them and what areas need improved. Revisit Part 5 to review which leadership styles you decided best fit your natural personality. You will begin to add to that and shape it and determine how leadership will specifically fit into your plan.

In the leadership sections of the program you were asked to explore your personal leadership style. Recall now what you answered when asked earlier in the program what you believe a phenomenal leader is made of. What did you write? Copy your answer exactly or re-word it, or you may even change your answer in some way.

What makes a phenomenal leader, in your opinion?

Next, you were asked in what ways you would like to improve your own personal leadership skills. I want to know how you have begun to improve those skills just in the time between first answering that question earlier in this book and now.

How have you taken steps to improve your personal leadership skills? What would you still like to improve as a leader?

You circled various examples of what a leader may look like, not physically, but examples of visible leadership. Take a moment to look back to that list and reflect on what leadership is, how it is viewed, what leaders do to gain that title, etc.

Write down some of the items you circled from that list, then write down how you intend on becoming that person, that visible leader.

In Part 5, you pinpointed what style(s) of leader you most resemble.

Which style, or styles, did you feel matched you most naturally? List them below:

It is important to not only grow and shape your leadership abilities, but to understand how your role as a leader fits directly into your specific life goals, steps to take to reach success, and your own happiness. Using all you have gathered and reflected on regarding your own strengths and weaknesses as a leader, as well as your own personal leadership style, generate a list of specific ways you will need to use those along your road map paths. Try keeping in mind leaders you personally know or know of and respect. You can learn from them and even mimic respectable behaviors in your own setting.

Lead the Way, Captain!

What style/type of leader did you decide you are?

List specific instances you will be required or it will be useful to step into that leadership role in your process to reaching the goal you have listed:

How do you foresee your role as a leader in the future?

Part 13

Incorporate Necessary Tools

Respect

One of the toughest but most mature things you can do is continue giving respect to others even when someone disrespects you. Maintaining class, kindness, and dignity in the moments others choose to display disrespect speaks volumes to you as a person. It isn't an easy trait and often takes self-motivation and intention, but we are all capable of maintaining a level temper in those situations. It certainly isn't acceptable to allow others to take advantage of you, repeatedly treat you poorly, or degrade you in any way, and I always encourage standing up for yourself. However, gaining and giving respect includes standing up for yourself with a sensible amount of pride and dignity and doing so without lowering yourself to a level where you are in return degrading someone, disrespecting them, or taking advantage.

As you travel through your life, checking off goals as you go, challenging yourself, and experiencing triumphs, setbacks, and heartache, one thing that you are capable of steadily maintaining throughout is your name, your persona, your reputation. No matter what happens to you, whether beyond any one person's control, caused by a person, good, bad, whatever happens to you, you have the strength and capability of maintaining a positive reputation. If you have positive and selfless goals, act with honesty and dignity, and are a genuinely good person, your reputation and the respect others have for you will never deceive you. In fact, a positive reputation can oftentimes come to your rescue in those moments where failure seemingly lurks at your doorstep. Living with dignity and respect, doing good and being good, is something others recognize and support, so if devastation arises or your challenges become too tough for you to handle alone, those whose support you have earned will almost always be there for you.

As you move through life, achieving goals, challenging yourself, growing and changing, and living your dreams, you will encounter numerous examples of respect (or lack of), which you can observe and learn from. Use all you learn to continuously shape yourself. I want you to flip back to Part 6 of this book, the chapter on respect, and review the positive intentions you circled and noted as things you would like to incorporate in your life.

Which intentions did you circle that you still believe you should and could use to help improve your life?

Now, begin incorporating intentional opportunities to give and gain respect in the steps you are taking to find success and happiness.

Always keep your eyes open for opportunities to respect others, build them up, learn from yourself and them. Even if you haven't had the best reputation in the past, even if you haven't been the nicest person, the classiest person, even if you aren't as traditionally educated as the person next to you, you deserve respect and are capable of giving it. Keep practicing and using those little daily moments that lend themselves to showing and gaining respect, and reflect on your growth as a person often so you can continue earning respect.

Respect

Reflect on your current life-this moment, right now. Are you respected? Are you respectful? Write your thoughts:

Using your knowledge of what it takes to be respectful and gain respect, create a list of ways you can (starting now) grow your reputation in a positive way by giving and gaining respect:

Part 14

Incorporate Necessary Tools

Share Greatness

I used to be afraid to share my thoughts, my projects, my ideas with others for fear of them being stolen or replicated, and for fear of embarrassment. What if no one liked my ideas? What if they made fun of me for thinking differently? What if my unique thoughts were stolen? What I have since learned is that sharing unique greatness, whether thoughts, ideas, inventions, or talents generates a feeling of true happiness and joy. For example, my boutique operates with a very unique mission and purpose. I was afraid to share the purpose of Amerie, the brands we carry, and all of our great services for fear that other boutiques would begin to copycat them. I now realize the more people who shop from my store or the more stores who begin carrying ethical brands like the ones carried in Amerie, the broader the impact will be on the world. Now, all I wish and work for is for everyone to know about our ethical brands and for more and more people to educate themselves, shop from these brands, and help spread the positive impact being made! If other boutiques begin carrying the same ethical brands as I do it would obviously create more competition and potentially affect sales, but it will also mean more lives being positively changed. It is a balance and allowing the good to outweigh the negative will inevitably end happily. It brings me joy to educate others, talk about the artisans whose items we carry, and continuously grow, change, and spread the mission. Whatever your dreams, your goals, whatever you are working toward, sharing it with others, while scary, can also bring joy and happiness to yourself and to them. The only way to spread your joy, your impact, your purpose is to share it. Like a young child sharing a toy, there is a chance your toy will be mistreated, damaged, or even stolen, but that doesn't happen every time. When it does happen, the poor actions can be corrected and will almost always be noticed. In the end, you were the one who did the right thing by taking a chance to share! It's worth it.

Let others into your mind just a little bit, let them be a part of your life story, and you may be surprised at how it makes you feel. Building bonds and connections with others the way I do when I educate a new customer or communicate with brand representatives, the way you would if you were working toward opening a business or writing a book, getting a promotion allows you to create lifelong connections, network, and grow your support team. You're allowed to be scared, expected to even, but you can't keep your ideas and goals hidden away completely. To start, try telling someone you trust about your goals. Saying them out loud to someone helps hold you more accountable and likely to accomplish them! Be proud of the work you are doing to better yourself. Do you hope to finally apply to colleges, earn your G.E.D., or work for a promotion? Whatever it is, tell someone, tell people, and when they see you really are working hard to reach that goal and are bettering yourself as a human in the process, they will want to be a part of it and provide whatever support they can. Let the world see who you are, leave a legacy, take ownership of your work, accomplishments, and dreams. Will everyone agree and share the same opinions as you? No. Will people judge you or disagree? Possibly. Someone will listen and support you, though, and that is where your attention should be spent.

You probably already have someone or a few people, maybe even a large following of people in mind as those who will automatically support your intentions. I want you to begin building your support team by starting with those people who are already part of your team and will take little convincing to get on board with your goals. Then, slowly think of others you are willing to work for to get on your team.

For example: Mom may be a shoe in for team captain of your support team, and best friend may be too, but you want to get co-workers or a boss on board, you want a teacher or mentor to be on board. It is never too soon to think about whose support you need.

With that said, think now of the variety of people you can recruit to your support team and share your goals and intentions with, maybe they will be inspired to do the same! Then you will need to begin considering who else could be positive and useful in your journey. Think of community members, acquaintances who you can reconnect with who would prove useful. Use the guide and space below to get started, but be sure to revisit your list often to continuously grow your network.

Super Support
Team Roster

List family and friends who you feel comfortable sharing your ideas and mission with and who will support you no matter what, and briefly identify how their involvement will benefit you:

Who are others you would like to rally to join your team? List them, tell how their involvement will prove beneficial, and jot ideas on how you plan to get their attention:

Part 15

Go Forth and Rise!

You have the tools you need to move forward toward your goals, to reach your success, to live happily. You actually had them all along. As you now know there are many facets to generating peace of mind and joy, but you were probably already aware of most of them and now you can go forth to better and better yourself.

I sometimes project a seemingly harsh tough love attitude to those I am closest with. I certainly don't intend to seem rude or hateful, rather I care so much and know what it takes to move past something or to get what I want and need that I want everyone to understand that same thing. I want to give you that same push. I am passionate about helping others, but oftentimes the help we need is actually something we must put into motion ourselves. As a teacher I cared greatly for my students, and they knew I cared for them. I was a tough teacher, though, and some students would believe me too harsh until realizing my intentions behind that toughness, which were for them to make necessary changes to better themselves. I hated seeing a student upset or defeated, for example, but sometimes a student would be bummed because of a poor test score or assignment grade. It may seem harsh especially for sixth grade students, but I tried to teach them that pouting, whining, or allowing a low score to defeat them was unacceptable. It took a lot to explain and demonstrate it, but my students eventually understood that the grades weren't up to me, the teacher. If they were unhappy with a score it was up to them to correct it, and I was there to guide them and help them do that. Once they realized that every single student was capable of receiving high scores if they used their personal potential and worked hard, they were able to use the tools to excel far beyond what most kids their ages accomplish. It was an amazing thing to witness, and I knew I had done my job, not just to teach grammar or writing skills, but to teach the students how to better themselves in all areas of school and life, a skill they can use throughout their entire lives.

It is the exact same with many adults. I have friends who allow a tough time or experience to completely depress them. I will be the first to understand and tell you that many experiences in life are out of our control, but how we react to them is totally in our hands. Tough love. Stop pouting, stop crying, stop feeling sorry for yourself. You have the ability to move past anything. You have the ability to come out an even better person, wiser, stronger. You have the ability to create something new and better from the ashes of tragedy or failure. It isn't easy, and it can sometimes take time and even more heartache or pain to get to that place where you can breathe and smile, but you can and will do it. It is a choice that is completely up to you.

Like when you were a young child, it is okay to fall, get hurt, get back up and, though hesitant and even fearful, try again. I'm pretty sure I fell more than once when learning to ice skate, or ride a bike, or tumble at gymnastics, but I eventually excelled at each of those because I got back up and tried again. It is supposed to be scary after you are hurt to try that same task again, but that is how we learn. It is no different in life. It is scary to go to college, scary to apply for a job or promotion, scary to open a business. Life experiences are scary, but if you allow fear to restrain you, what will you do in life? Nothing at all, and you may regret that when it's too late. I'm scared right now writing this book, or anytime I write a book. What will people think? What negative responses will readers have to my words? It is scary, and there is a chance someone will say hateful things about my book, but there is an equal chance that someone will respond positively. That, the positive, is what I choose to focus on. Go for it, and let the negatives come, but soak the positives in. I have learned to listen to the negatives just enough to decide whether they are actually useful in my self-improvement or just unnecessary negatives. Keep what is useful and toss the rest aside. If I inspired one person through my writing, none of the negatives matter, and that is how I want you to approach your tasks.

Every single person deserves to experience happiness and a feeling of accomplishment and pride, but if you never do the things that will allow you to feel that way, it will never be possible. Use the tools you have within and the ones I have given you and go forth to find happiness! What will people say about you long from now when you are gone? What do you want them to say? Whatever it is, it is possible. You can and you will!

So, what's next? You have read and reflected on various aspects of your habits, routines, and your life. Now, all you have to do is piece those together to generate a plan of action. If you want to open a business, use what you have learned to build your skills and begin working toward that goal. If you are hoping to become eligible for a promotion at work, use what you have learned to better yourself and make yourself the best possible candidate for that promotion. Whatever it is that you desire deep within, you are capable of accomplishing it! Take what you have learned and remember it is a continuous growth process. Get excited about the ever growing and changing you! Get excited about knowing you can accomplish things you never thought possible. Get excited and put in the work. You will find that it was all worth it!

I suggest using the journal spaces remaining to plan. If you like to make lists, make a list. If you prefer doodling or drawing your ideas or roadmap thoughts, do that! Use the spaces however you wish, but please never give up. You will find random thoughts, truly random thoughts throughout the journal pages. Read them or don't. Sometimes I find it useful to let my mind wander in deep thought on haphazard thoughts. It can often help generate new useful thoughts. Now, go forth and rise to the challenge!

Use this space to make a plan, write your thoughts, and conquer!

Use this space to make a plan, write your thoughts, and conquer!
Random thought: Amerie Boutique (my small business)
carries clothing, accessories, and gifts from ethical brands
that give back. What if every customer at Amerie donated
$1 during each visit? That would add upwards of $20,000
extra for the charity organizations we support!
What small gesture can you make that would make a big impact?

Use this space to make a plan, write your thoughts, and conquer!

Use this space to make a plan, write your thoughts, and conquer!

Use this space to make a plan, write your thoughts, and conquer!

Use this space to make a plan, write your thoughts, and conquer!

Use this space to make a plan, write your thoughts, and conquer!

Use this space to make a plan, write your thoughts, and conquer!

Random thought: Remember reading the phrase, "I can. I will!" in different sections of this book? Don't forget it! ***What have you done so far to move nearer to your goals?***

Use this space to make a plan, write your thoughts, and conquer!

Use this space to make a plan, write your thoughts, and conquer!

Use this space to make a plan, write your thoughts, and conquer!

Use this space to make a plan, write your thoughts, and conquer!

Use this space to make a plan, write your thoughts, and conquer!

Random thought: If everyone thought the same way, and handled experiences the exact same, we would never have opportunities to learn from one another. **What are your thoughts on that?**

Use this space to make a plan, write your thoughts, and conquer!

Use this space to make a plan, write your thoughts, and conquer!

Use this space to make a plan, write your thoughts, and conquer!

Use this space to make a plan, write your thoughts, and conquer!
Random thought: Do you know what Fair Trade is? If not, look it up.
Once you do, write your thoughts on it here:

Use this space to make a plan, write your thoughts, and conquer!

Use this space to make a plan, write your thoughts, and conquer!

Use this space to make a plan, write your thoughts, and conquer!

Use this space to make a plan, write your thoughts, and conquer!

Use this space to make a plan, write your thoughts, and conquer!

Use this space to make a plan, write your thoughts, and conquer!

Use this space to make a plan, write your thoughts, and conquer!

Random thought: what is something you whined or complained about this week? For example, I thought to myself, "Man, I wish I had better water pressure in my shower. My showers would be so much more relaxing if I had better pressure." Then I realized there are people in the world who would love nothing more than a bowl full of clean water, and I pushed the trivial thought aside.

Random thought: Put your eggs somewhere safe when traveling home from the grocery store. I would hate for them to fall and break! Okay, this was a really random thought, but little mannerisms and habits say a lot about a person. How do you pack your eggs to travel from the grocery store?

Use this space to make a plan, write your thoughts, and conquer!

Use this space to make a plan, write your thoughts, and conquer!

Use this space to make a plan, write your thoughts, and conquer!

Use this space to make a plan, write your thoughts, and conquer!

Use this space to make a plan, write your thoughts, and conquer!

Use this space to make a plan, write your thoughts, and conquer!

Use this space to make a plan, write your thoughts, and conquer!

Use this space to make a plan, write your thoughts, and conquer!

Use this space to make a plan, write your thoughts, and conquer!

Random Thought: Have you ever lost a loved one? I've lost a few, whether from death or just from leaving my life, losing a loved one is tough. Write about your experience. How did it make you feel? How did you cope? Is there anything you would do differently on your part?

Use this space to make a plan, write your thoughts, and conquer!

Use this space to make a plan, write your thoughts, and conquer!

Use this space to make a plan, write your thoughts, and conquer!

Use this space to make a plan, write your thoughts, and conquer!

Never give up! Always keep working toward bettering yourself, your life, and reaching your goals. Every person is capable of happiness and success no matter their background. You can do this!

Visit www.ginamullis.com for more tips, tricks, and guidance!

About the Author

Gina began writing books during her first teaching job and published the fiction fantasy, Friedenland, in 2013. She went on to teach for six and a half years before her life-changing Multiple Sclerosis diagnosis. After the news, Gina decided to take control of her life regardless of the incurable disease and opened her own small business. Amerie Cause-Supporting Boutique provides unique brands that give back, which is Gina's dream in life: to help others. Using those experiences, Gina now acts as an active community leader, entrepreneur, speaker, and motivator. She enjoys traveling to speak to students and business teams, volunteering with numerous organizations, and meeting amazing people.

Gina has a passion for health and fitness, animals (especially her kitty, Alaska), writing, and educating others on ways to help others. She earned her Bachelor's degree in English Education from the University of Southern Indiana and holds a Master's degree in Education.

Printed in the United States
By Bookmasters